No One Can Take
Your Place

Sheri Dew

**DESERET
BOOK**

SALT LAKE CITY, UTAH

Library of Congress Cataloging-in-Publication Data

Dew, Sheri L.
  No one can take your place / Sheri Dew.
    p.   cm.
  Includes index.
  ISBN 1-59038-181-5 (hardcover : alk. paper)
  1. Spiritual life—Church of Jesus Christ of Latter-day Saints. 2. Church of Jesus Christ of Latter-day Saints—Doctrines. I. Title.
  BX8656.D48 2004
  248.4'89332—dc22
                            2004017132

Printed in the United States of America   72076
Publishers Printing, Salt Lake City, UT

10   9   8   7   6   5   4   3   2   1

Contents

We Are Men and Women of God

CHAPTER ONE

We Will Not Flinch

Premortally, in the most difficult of circumstances,
we stood loyally by our Father and His Son,
and we did not flinch. The question for us today is:
How will we do it again?

I HATE SNAKES. No, let me restate that: I am terrified of snakes. Traumatized by snakes. Completely undone by snakes. My fear got so bad when I was growing up that whenever there was a snake-sighting on our Kansas farm, Mother would instruct my siblings not to tell me—because even the knowledge that the slimy critters had been spotted in the vicinity was enough to keep me indoors. Embarrassing as it is to admit it, this phobia is so extreme that it is one of the few things that limits where I'm willing to go or walk or hike. There just isn't much that's worth risking the possibility of running into a snake.

Just recently I had knee surgery, and as soon as my knee would allow I began taking long walks, cane in hand, to try to regain the strength and flexibility in my knee. One day a friend and I set off on an early-morning walk, and at one point I suggested we follow a trail that went into the foothills near my home. We were chatting about this and that, enjoying a beautiful, clear summer morning. I was just ready to tell my friend I thought my knee had gone about as far as it was going to make it, when suddenly, dead ahead in the trail, I saw something sinister begin to coil. I instantly screamed, "Rattlesnake!" and then began the fastest exit you've ever seen by a middle-aged woman recovering from knee surgery. As I hopped and half-ran back down the path, I was trembling. And for days, each time that disgusting image came to mind, it made me shiver and react all over again.

I couldn't help but think about that experience when I recently came across a statement by President George Q. Cannon. He said that when Satan unleashed his fury against the Father and the Son in the premortal world and was cast out of heaven, we who are here today "stood loyally by God and by Jesus, and . . . did not flinch" (*Gospel Truth*, 7).

Webster defines *flinch* as "to shrink from" or "to tense involuntarily in fear." I guarantee that I did more than tense involuntarily in fear when I saw that snake, which is not only a creepy creature but to me symbolizes all that is evil.

There are a lot of things in the world today that ought to make us flinch, things from which we ought to shrink—distractions, deceptions, and snares inspired by Satan for the express purpose of trapping and derailing us. But on the other hand, once again, as Satan increasingly unleashes his fury against the Father and the Son, by unleashing his fury against all who are determined to "stand as witnesses of God at all times and in all things, and in all places" (Mosiah 18:9), we have the challenge of doing again what we have done before—of standing loyally by God and by Jesus and not flinching even in the face of the onslaught.

Bottom line: Premortally, in the most difficult of circumstances, we stood loyally by our Father and His Son, and we did not flinch. The question for us today is: How will we do it again?

For starters, we would be wise to see how those who've gone before us managed the same challenge. The scriptures are replete with examples of faithful, determined, committed men and women who did not flinch. Moses' encounter with Lucifer is a perfect example. Four times the adversary tried to tempt and deceive Moses: "Satan came tempting him, saying: Moses, son of man, worship me" (Moses 1:12). But because Moses had earlier had a spectacular experience with God, he could easily distinguish between God and Satan, so he wasn't fooled. "Get thee hence, Satan; deceive me not," he responded. "I will not cease to call upon God, I have other things to inquire of him: for his glory has been upon me, wherefore I can judge between him and thee. Depart hence, Satan" (Moses 1:16, 18).

But Satan didn't stop there. He ranted and railed, enough that Moses feared exceedingly. "Nevertheless, calling upon God, [Moses] received strength, and he commanded, saying: Depart from me, Satan, for this one God only will I worship, which is the God of glory" (Moses 1:20).

Yet a third and a fourth time Moses had to command Lucifer to leave, but because Moses stood firm and did not flinch in the face of terrifying evil, commanding him in the name of the Only Begotten to depart, Satan had no option but to leave.

Moses did not flinch. He didn't flinch because he could distinguish between good and evil. He detected Satan right off the bat and stood firm against him. He was strong because he knew what power to call upon to deliver him from evil.

Abinadi didn't flinch either, when he was taken before King Noah. Pressed to deny that Christ would come, he responded: "I will not recall the words which I have spoken concerning this people, for they are true; and that ye may know of their surety I have suffered myself that I have fallen into your hands. Yea, and I will suffer even until death, and I will not recall my words, and they shall stand as a testimony against you" (Mosiah 17:9–10).

Abinadi did not recall his words. He died a martyr's death. Because he had an impenetrable witness of the coming of Jesus Christ, he stood firm.

Jacob didn't flinch when confronted by the articulate, intelligent Sherem, the anti-Christ, who knew how to draw upon the power of the devil (see Jacob 7:4). Jacob wasn't confused, distracted, or deceived. By his own account he explained why: "And [Sherem] had hope to shake me from the faith, notwithstanding the many revelations and the many things which I had seen . . . for I truly had seen angels, and they had ministered unto me. And also, I had heard the voice of the Lord speaking unto me in very word, from time to time; wherefore, I could not be shaken" (Jacob 7:5).

The list of noble men and women who have stood firm in the face of frightening evils, temptations, or mortal obstacles goes on and on. Many more will be identified throughout the pages of this book—many who "with unwearyingness declared the word" (Helaman 10:4) and who were "no less serviceable" (Alma 48:19), who stood loyally by God and by Jesus and did not flinch. They all had something in common: They believed in Jesus Christ. They understood the fundamental doctrines of the gospel, including where and how to turn for help. And they knew *how* to draw upon the power of God.

The questions for us are fairly simple: Do we have an impenetrable testimony of Jesus Christ? Do we know where and how to turn for help? Do we know how to draw upon the power of God? Do we understand how magnificent and how encompassing the doctrines of the gospel really are?

Not long ago I heard President Gordon B. Hinckley declare, simply, "I just wish I could tell the whole world what we believe. Because the gospel makes so much sense!"

I thought about this recently during a trip to New York City. My work has taken me to that city dozens of times, and as a result I've been to Central Park many times. I've taken walks there, introduced family and friends to favorite spots, and basically just enjoyed this rather remarkable stretch of green in the middle of a concrete jungle. And frankly, as lovely as the park was, I always felt New Yorkers made a little too much of it. I'd reached the conclusion that they prized it so much because it was the only grass in Manhattan.

But on this trip something unusual happened. One day I had the morning free, and I headed out to walk/jog through Central Park. Because I wasn't pressed for time, I took a different route than I'd taken before—one that took me right into the center of the park. I walked and jogged, walked and jogged, walked and jogged—and the deeper into the park I went, the more amazed I became. I had never seen half of what was there. I hadn't known there was a castle in Central Park. I'd never eaten at the Boathouse or jogged around the reservoir, or seen a hundred other things that I saw for the first time that day. It was bigger than I thought; there were far more things to do than I had realized. At first,

I couldn't quite figure out what had happened—until I bought a map of the park. As it turns out, on the dozens of visits earlier, I had basically just cut across the various corners and walked along the edges. I'd never gone right down through the middle. And what I found by doing so changed my view of the park forever. It was far, far more than I had ever realized. I can see now why New Yorkers make such a big deal of Central Park. It *is* a big deal.

As you read the pages in this book, I invite you to consider if you may have cut across the corners and walked along the edges of the gospel and the word of God, or if you have charged right down through the middle of the doctrine. Have you begun to discover the joy and potential that result from knowing and pondering and understanding what we believe? Is it possible that there is more—perhaps much more—to what the Lord has revealed than you currently understand?

The more we know and understand, the more useful we are to the Lord. For "the glory of God is intelligence, or, in other words, light and truth," and "light and truth forsake that evil one" (D&C 93:36–37).

With that in mind, here are a few questions we may all wish to consider as we study and ponder the word of God:

Do we know how to get answers to prayer, how to receive personal revelation? (2 Nephi 32, Alma 17, D&C 93, and D&C 76 are great places to begin.)

Do we understand that when we leave the temple we emerge armed with power, what kind of power it is, and how we gain access to that power? (See D&C 109.)

Do we know that the power of Jesus Christ is greater than any power Satan can muster? (See Moses 1; D&C 50.)

Do we understand who we are? Do we know if the phrase "the

noble and great ones" (Abraham 3; D&C 138) has anything to do with us?

Do we understand, have we experienced for ourselves, that the Atonement can heal our broken hearts, can help us turn our mortal weakness into strength? (See Luke 4; Ether 12; Alma 11.)

Do we understand why sexual purity is so important to the Lord, and why He feels so strongly about marriage and the family unit? (See Jacob 2–3.)

The gospel of Jesus Christ is filled with so much depth and breadth and richness. Sometimes, I fear, we're a bit ho-hum about what we know and have and enjoy. Is there any chance C. S. Lewis was describing us when he mused in this oft-quoted reflection: "We are half-hearted creatures, fooling about with drink and sex and ambition when infinite joy is offered us, like an ignorant child who wants to go on making mud pies in the slum because he cannot imagine what is meant by an offer of a holiday at the sea. . . . We are far too easily pleased" (*A Mind Awake,* 168).

I had the privilege of assisting with the VIP tours conducted prior to the public tours of the new Manhattan New York Temple. One day I took the executive team of an international financial institution through the temple, along the way explaining briefly the purpose of temples and why they are so sacred to us. In one of the rooms I explained that not only do we believe in life after death but we believe there is a dynamic connection between the lives we live here and where and how we will live after we die.

One member of that executive team was a tall, handsome man who seemed quite thoughtful throughout the tour. Afterward he said: "You know, what you've taught here makes so much sense. I have two teenage boys who are good boys, but I've had a hard time convincing them that there is really any reason to be good and to live a certain way. But I can see that if they understood that what they do here has major ramifications later, it could make all the difference."

A light had turned on for this man—the light about something exquisitely sublime and reassuring, yet so fundamentally simple that we may take it for granted at times.

Again, in the words of President Hinckley, "the gospel makes so much sense!" It is the "oil of gladness" (Hebrews 1:9). It is the good news. And the more we probe its depth and breadth, the more likely we will be able, regardless of the opposition, to once again stand loyally by God and by Jesus, and to do so without so much as even flinching at the onslaught of the world.

What Nephi taught is true: If we will "press forward, feasting upon the word of Christ, and endure to the end, . . . [we] shall have eternal life" (2 Nephi 31:20).

And that is because we will not flinch.

CHAPTER TWO

Eve and Mary: Exemplars for the Ages

Nothing was left to chance for Eve and Mary,
and neither is it left to chance for us. There is not a man or
woman in this Church who doesn't have a specific mission
to perform in helping build up the kingdom of God.

RECENTLY, A YOUNG WOMAN gave me a compliment after I had finished speaking that I didn't deserve but that made me laugh right out loud. "Sister Dew," she said, "every morning when you wake up I'll bet the adversary says to himself, 'Oh heck, she's awake again.'" Her comment not only gave me a new daily goal and objective but prompted me to ponder the fact that we who are here now, in the last wave of laborers in the Lord's vineyard (see D&C 33:3), have been born now for very specific reasons. Yes, we're here to receive bodies and ordinances and to be tested. But the doctrine seems to be clear about the fact that, for us, it goes even further. We know that our Father has held us in reserve until the latter part of the latter days—that, in fact, as President George Q. Cannon expressed it, he held those in reserve who would have the courage and the determination to face the world and all the powers of the evil one and to yet be fearless in building Zion (see *Gospel Truth*, 18).

Be fearless in building Zion. That's quite a statement, and quite a responsibility. And yet it is not unlike something President Gordon B. Hinckley taught in his April 2004 general conference address: "Our times are fraught with peril. . . . But peril is not a new condition for the human family. Revelation tells us that 'there was war in heaven.' . . . What a perilous time that must have been. The Almighty Himself was pitted against the son of the morning. We were there while that was going on. That must have been a desperately difficult struggle, with a grand, triumphal victory. . . . Why were we then happy? I think it was because . . . we turned our backs on the adversary and aligned ourselves with the forces of God, and those forces were victorious" ("Dawning of a Brighter Day," 81).

The forces of God will again be victorious, despite the perilous time in which we live. And God will be victorious in part because of each of us. Joseph Smith's translation of the verse "Seek ye first the kingdom of God, and his righteousness" (Matthew 6:33) adds five clarifying words that spell out our mission: "Seek ye first *to build up* the kingdom of God, and *to establish* his righteousness" (JST, Matthew 6:38).

Here is the simple, sobering, spine-tingling truth: By virtue of who we are, what we know, the covenants we have made, and the fact that we are here now, *we were born to help build up the kingdom of God!* As mothers and grandmothers, fathers and grandfathers, sisters and brothers and friends and teachers and colleagues who will defend truth in every setting, *we were born to be a light and a "standard for the nations"* (D&C 115:5). *We were born to open our mouths* and declare the gospel "with the sound of rejoicing" (D&C 28:16). And yes, like the Prophet Joseph, in this time fraught with peril we were even born to be disturbers and annoyers of the adversary's kingdom (see Joseph Smith–History 1:20).

Because of the complex, convoluted, confounded time in which we live, our assignment is *not* easy. So, how *will* we do what we agreed long ago to do?

The Savior has marked the path and shown us the way. But in addition, valiant men and women through the ages have proven that mortality can be mastered.

I have grown up with my own set of scriptural heroes—probably just like you have. Captain Moroni is my kind of man. I love his style. And then there's Nephi; how can you not take note of all that Nephi experienced and endured? And the boy Mormon. And his son Moroni. And Alma and Ammon. And Abinadi and Amulek. And Paul. And the list goes on and on. Each of them, and countless others, have shown their mettle under the most confusing and trying of circumstances. They too have lived in times fraught with peril.

But because we so often single out scriptural heroes rather than heroines, I have chosen in this chapter to refer specifically to two glorious women who are, for me, the two greatest heroines of all time. They are two women upon whom the entire plan of salvation depended: Eve, whose choice in Eden initiated the Fall; and Mary, who was worthy and willing to bear the mortal Messiah. Both were firsts, elected to go where no woman had gone before.

According to our Father's plan, we had to fall. And we had to have a Redeemer. Mary and Eve were pivotal to both. Yet, it is not the drama of their duties that inspires me. It is the simple fact that, under staggering circumstances and with the fate of the human family hanging in the balance, they did what they were sent here to do.

We do not worship Mary or Eve. They were mortals, not gods. But we may safely look to them to see where they looked, to see how they dealt with the impossible, and to identify God-given attributes we all have that we need to awaken within ourselves if we are going to do what *we* have been sent here to do—attributes such as faith, knowledge, obedience, purity, integrity, a clear sense of identity, and courage.

Faith. Mary and Eve had unwavering faith in God the Father and His Son Jesus Christ.

Consider Adam and Eve's challenge. *Prior* to being introduced into mortality, they were commanded to "multiply, and replenish the earth" (Moses 2:28). Yet they were placed in the Garden in a state in which they could not have children. Hence the imperative need for a Fall that would result in posterity as well as mortality and death.

Our eternal destiny hung on Adam and Eve's faith in the Plan and their willingness to obey the command to multiply. President Joseph Fielding Smith said this: "I never speak of the part Eve took in this fall as a sin, nor do I accuse Adam of a sin. . . . This was a transgression of the law, but not a sin . . . for it was something that Adam and Eve had to do!" (*Doctrines of Salvation,* 1:114–15). Elder John A. Widtsoe added that the problem before Adam and Eve was whether "to remain forever at selfish ease in the Garden of Eden, or to face unselfishly tribulation and death, in bringing to pass the purposes of the Lord for a host of waiting spirit children. They chose the latter. This they did with open eyes and minds as to consequences. . . . The choice that they made raises Adam and Eve to pre-eminence among all who have come on earth" (*Evidences and Reconciliations*, 193–94). What monumental faith by the mother of all living!

Mary's faith was equally remarkable. She was stunned when Gabriel announced that she would bear the Christ Child. But her response—"Behold the handmaid of the Lord; be it unto me according to thy word" (Luke 1:38)—compares in terms of submission to that which her Son would utter later in Gethsemane: "Nevertheless not my will, but thine, be done" (Luke 22:42). Imagine also the faith required to mother the Son of God. Surely at times Mary felt a crushing sense of inadequacy—which could only be managed with faith. But she pondered sacred things in her heart (see Luke 2:19, 51), which no doubt helped bolster and continually strengthen her faith.

Faith is the first principle of the gospel for good reason. For it is our faith—our fervent trust that the Father and the Son will do for us what they have promised to do—that unlocks the power of the Atonement and the promise of eternal life in our lives. The very Restoration was undertaken so "that faith . . . might increase in the earth" (D&C 1:21). There is nothing we need more than to increase our faith. Few of us doubt that the Lord *can* help us. Our question is usually: But will He help *me*?

During the recent past, I have faced a baffling challenge that has tested my faith and my spiritual mettle all over again. I've worked and fasted and pleaded for help. But the answers haven't come easily or quickly. At times things have looked hopeless—until I have asked myself one question: "Sheri, do you believe the Lord will help you, or don't you?"

That question always stops me short. Because I do believe. I believe He will help because He always has. He hasn't always given me everything I've prayed for—far from it—but He has never let me down. He always helps me and gives me what I need. And every time I undergo another divine tutorial, it increases my reservoir of faith for the next challenge. As hard as it is, I am grateful every time my faith is stretched, because *only* if our testimony of Jesus Christ penetrates every aspect of our lives will we be able to do what we have come here to do.

Knowledge. Mary and Eve understood the doctrine. There is no finer sentence sermon on the plan of happiness than Eve's: "Were it not for our transgression we never should have had seed, and never should have known good and evil, and the joy of our redemption, and the eternal life which God giveth unto all the obedient" (Moses 5:11).

Likewise, Mary's sublime doctrinal soliloquy that begins, "My soul doth magnify the Lord, And my spirit hath rejoiced in God my Saviour" (Luke 1:46–47), revealed that she clearly understood the work, character, love, and mission of the Son she was carrying.

These women knew the doctrine. They had to. Adam and Eve were the only ones who could make "all things known unto their sons and their daughters" (Moses 5:12), and Mary was entrusted with nurturing the boy Jesus. Both Mary and Eve taught, testified, and prophesied. Their knowledge undergirded their faith, because in order to produce results, faith must be based upon truth.

Not long ago I was racing through security in a major airport when I was pulled aside for an extra search. The officer opened my briefcase, pulled out my scriptures, replaced them, handed me my bag, and said with a thick but charming accent, "I do not worry about the people who have this book."

I don't worry either about those who have allowed the truths in the books that contain the word of God to penetrate their hearts and minds and lives. They know who they are and why they're here. They know how to detect even subtle distortions of truth. They know where and how to turn for peace, strength, and guidance. They cannot resist repenting. And they know not only what the Lord has promised He will do, but that He will do it for them.

So, do we know the doctrine? If, for example, we don't understand the spiritual gifts that are available to us, it is unlikely we'll be able to cultivate and draw upon them. Speaking of the vision described in the 76th section of the Doctrine and Covenants, Joseph Smith declared: "I could explain a hundred fold more than I ever have of the glories of the kingdoms manifested to me in the vision, were I permitted, and were the people prepared to receive them" (*Teachings of the Prophet Joseph Smith,* 305). Imagine! A hundred fold more than the magnificent truths revealed in Section 76? This prompts the natural question, Do we know what's in Section 76? And a follow-up question: What would we need to do or know or show for the Prophet to feel we were ready to learn and understand more?

We know that "whatever principle of intelligence we attain . . . in this life . . . will rise with us in the resurrection" (D&C 130:18), but it also helps while we're here. Recently a friend lamented that she can't remember half of the scriptures she studies. "But I've decided it's my job to put them in," she said, "and the Holy Ghost's job to pull them out when I need them." There is some truth to that.

Keep in mind that the greatest source of knowledge is the temple, where we learn more about who we are, who the Lord is, who the adversary is, and how to draw upon the powers of heaven to draw near to the Savior and in the process forsake Satan. The more we know, the more our faith will increase, the more likely that when we open our

mouths, the Holy Ghost will have something to work with, and thus
the more useful we will be in building the kingdom.

Obedience. Mary and Eve were models of obedience. At Gabriel's
dramatic announcement, Mary asked in wonder, "How shall this be,
seeing I know not a man?" (Luke 1:34). But after angelic reassurance,
she doubted no more and demonstrated total obedience.

Likewise, after being banished from the presence of God, Adam and
Eve were "obedient unto the commandments of the Lord," they "ceased
not to call upon God," and they taught their children to obey (Moses
5:5; 5:16; 6:1). What devotion to obedience!

Satan tries to make sin look liberating and obedience look restric-
tive and unreasonable. But sin is never the easier way. A poignant experience reinforced this when one evening I accompanied a dear friend
who asked for support to a disciplinary council and there witnessed the
unconsolable remorse of someone fully aware of the consequences of
sin. I saw the anguish that accompanies the loss of membership in the
Church and all of those attendant gifts. Greater agony I have not seen.
Unrepented sin enslaves us to anguish. If I had a video of that experience, I'd never have to give another morality talk at a standards night. It
would speak for itself.

Elder Bruce R. McConkie said that "to be valiant in the testimony
of Jesus is to take the Lord's side on *every* issue" ("Be Valiant in the
Fight of Faith," 35; emphasis added). As a step toward greater obedience, we would each do well to take inventory of where we stand on
every issue about which the Lord or His servants have declared a
position—everything from modesty to the precision with which we
honor our temple covenants. A simple test applies to everything: Whose

agenda does it support, the Lord's or the adversary's? Discipleship requires escalating submission to the Lord.

For me, the best part of the Good News is that the Lord works with imperfect people—meaning all of us. Nothing brings more joy more quickly than precise obedience.

Purity. Other than Jesus Christ, there may not be a finer mortal example of purity than his mother, who prophets prophesied would be "beautiful and fair above all other virgins" (1 Nephi 11:15).

That Mary lived up to her premortal assignment was clear when Gabriel declared, "Blessed art thou among women . . . for thou hast found favour with God" (Luke 1:28, 30). Said Elder Bruce R. McConkie: "As there is only one Christ, so there is only one Mary. . . . [W]e may confidently conclude that [the Father] selected the most worthy and spiritually talented of all his spirit daughters to be the mortal mother of his Eternal Son" (*Doctrinal New Testament Commentary,* 1:85). To be worthy to bear the Son of God, Mary had to be pure. Not perfect, but pure—in thought, word, deed, and motive.

The object of this life is not to become perfect. Could we all just pledge to give that up once and for all! But it is to become increasingly pure, which will eventually lead to perfection.

We are the only ones who can show our young women and young men that it is possible to live with purity in a polluted world. We are the only ones who can show them that purity is not prudish and that vulgarity is not funny. And we are the only ones who can show them that a woman who has the Spirit with her is absolutely radiant, and a man of God who honors the priesthood he holds is the finest example of manhood to be found!

Obedience and repentance are the keys to purity, which will

increasingly distinguish men and women of God from the men and women of the world.

Integrity. Although Eve was fiercely obedient to the Lord's command to multiply and replenish the earth, she was also beguiled by Satan (see Moses 4:19). And yet, her response to what happened in the Garden was remarkable. She immediately acknowledged what she had done and accepted the consequences. She didn't lie. She didn't pout. She didn't get defensive. She didn't blame Adam. What humility and integrity from "our glorious Mother Eve"! (D&C 138:39.)

It is important to note that Satan had mixed a lie, "Ye shall not surely die," with the truth—"Your eyes shall be opened, and ye shall . . . [know] good and evil" (Moses 4:10–11). This is still Satan's game—to mix and muddle error and truth until we are hard-pressed to tell the difference.

Though we don't know the exact nature of her beguilement, we do know that Eve then instantly recognized Satan. And here is the eye-popping part—there is no scriptural evidence to suggest that she ever fell for his deceit again.

Like Eve, we too must learn to identify Satan, for his tactics against covenant-making men and women are sinister in their subtlety. I don't care how valiant or smart or talented a person is, no one is resilient enough to tango with Satan and survive. He is too experienced at spiritual ambush. One meaning of the name *Satan* is "the one who lies in wait" (Hugh Nibley, *Approaching Zion*, 92). And does he ever! Which is why the only way to deal with him—and to teach our youth to deal with him—is to shun him like the snake that he is and leave him *completely* alone.

Forsaking Satan may mean changing things. It may require changing wardrobes or changing channels or changing attitudes or changing habits or changing lifestyles or even changing friends, because it's not possible to *sort of* dress modestly or *kind of* tell the truth or act with integrity *most* of the time or *almost* be morally clean. Nine percent tithing isn't tithing, it's a donation.

Both Mary and Eve, whose lives of obedience are evidence of their total rejection of the adversary, demonstrated that it is possible to have the integrity to both recognize and entirely forsake Satan.

Identity. God named Eve the mother of all living *before* she was placed in the Garden (Moses 4:26), and He elected Mary to bear His Son *before* she entered mortality. Their identity and callings were determined long before they were born, and were surely a reflection of premortal spiritual valor. None of us come to this earth to *gain* our worth; we brought it with us.

Nothing was left to chance for Eve and Mary, and neither is it left to chance for us. Said President Wilford Woodruff, "The Lord has chosen a small number of choice spirits of sons and daughters out of all the creations of God, who are to inherit this earth; and this company of choice spirits have been kept in the spirit world for six thousand years to come forth in the last days . . . to build . . . up and to defend [the kingdom of God]" (*Our Lineage*, 4).

There is not a man or woman in this Church who doesn't have a specific mission to perform in helping build up the kingdom of God. And the more we come to *really believe* that, the more immune we become to the world's distractions.

I offer as Exhibit A the recent rash (or should I say "trash") of TV reality and game shows—*Survivor, The Weakest Link, American Idol,* and don't even get me started on *The Bachelor*—each of which crowns one lucky winner. These awful programs perpetuate the big fat lie that only one person can win. Satan, who is the quintessential exclusionist, loves to leave people out—probably because he knows he'll never be included in the only group that matters.

In stunning and striking contrast, our Father is staggeringly inclusive. *Every one* of us can be "joint-heirs with Christ" and receive *all* our Father has (Romans 8:17). Exaltation is for everyone who is wise in this agonizing, magnificent probation of ours (see Mormon 9:28).

That includes you, as one of those who have been reserved for this eleventh hour (see D&C 33:3). You are here now because you were divinely *elected* to be here now. The simple fact and plain truth is that Mary and Eve and countless other glorious women as well as countless magnificent men were *not* assigned to this dispensation. We were. It is humbling and a little scary. But do you think God would have left the last days to chance by sending men and women He couldn't depend on? There is *no chance* He would have been that cavalier or careless. The cumulative verdict of patriarchal blessings in our time is that we were sent now because some of the most trustworthy of our Father's children would be needed in the final decisive battle for righteousness. That is who we are, and it is who we have always been.

Now, Mary and Eve exemplified many other attributes that are core to our divine nature that we could address. Selflessness and wisdom, consecration and patience, and sheer endurance are some that come to mind. But we come now to the final, at least for our purposes in this chapter, and most compelling attribute, which is actually an outgrowth of all the others.

Courage. Eve's decision in the Garden was simply the most courageous any woman has ever made. Period! But that was neither the beginning nor the end of her courage. Imagine the courage to be the first female mortal pioneer. Then imagine the courage to face banishment and stand, side by side with her husband, as they tamed an unknown wilderness.

Mary's assignment was no less daunting. Espoused to Joseph, she was suddenly and, at least to most, unexplainably with child. Yet, her immediate response was both obedient and brave. And her challenges only began there. When others, choked with fear, abandoned Jesus, His mother stood by the cross. Both Mary and Eve had unflinching moral courage.

We too need unflinching moral courage. A recent experience demonstrated this vividly for me. To my great surprise, in March 2003 I found myself at the United Nations as a White House delegate to an international commission focused on issues relevant to women. The setting was entirely new and quite overwhelming. New people. New language, as it were. New motives to discern. And an entirely new system to understand.

From day one, I observed something that seemed curiously incongruous. Women who impressed me as God-fearing souls in search of honest solutions to their problems often lobbied for the same things as women who had blatantly evil designs. I struggled to know if there was a way, apart from spiritual discernment, to detect the motives of these women. I listened carefully to what these two varying groups said and at night searched the scriptures for insight. But it was a puzzle.

Then one evening as our U.S. delegation held a briefing, angry lobbyists began to attack us about the President's position on HIV/AIDS. These women were vicious. They were mean! In fact, if you don't mind me saying so, they were as unattractive (read: ugly) as any women I had ever met. As I prayed silently to know what to say when I took the podium, I had a clear impression: "Sheri, don't you see? The mean ones are the evil ones." My fear vanished instantly. Now that I knew how to identify those on the opposing side, I wasn't afraid, because I learned long ago that Satan never backs up his followers but the Master always does. The power of Jesus Christ is *always* stronger than any power emanating from the dark underbelly of the adversary. Believing the Lord would fill my mouth if I would just open it, I plunged in, at first uncertain how to both teach truth and support the administration.

As I began, I heard these words come out of my mouth: "The first point of President Bush's plan to fight AIDS is abstinence," I said. "Surely any reasonable person would agree that the only sure way to stop AIDS is for those who aren't infected to have no sexual relations with those who are." (I was tempted to say that they were looking at someone who'd had a whole lot of experience with abstinence and knew what she was talking about.) Several women looked ready to pounce. But I kept going.

"The next point is to be faithful to one partner in marriage. If sexual relations were restricted to husband and wife, AIDS would not spread." At that, two women attacked, but it didn't last long because their arguments were, frankly, idiotic. Remember, Satan abandons his prey. And then, the women who agreed with me began to cheer, silencing the attackers for good.

What did I learn at the U.N.? I learned that vigorous differences of opinion can be discussed respectfully, but when people become vicious, they are likely working for the adversary. I learned that even in a spiritually hostile environment, truth is truth, and there is power in truth. I learned that when we have faith in the Lord, we like Paul "may boldly say, The Lord is my helper, and I will not fear" (Hebrews 13:6). And I learned that the gospel is *so* practical. During two weeks I heard no issue debated that couldn't have been resolved by applying truth. The gospel of Jesus Christ has the answer to every conflict in our lives, our families, and even our nations. His truths heal hearts and bridge cultures.

And they also inspire courage. The courage to stand alone. The courage to open our mouths when prompted. The courage to prepare the greatest generation of missionaries, mentor the greatest generation of youth, and share the gospel in any setting. Unflinching moral courage.

Every time we exercise our faith in the face of fear or discover a doctrinal insight in the scriptures or the temple, we are better able to build the kingdom of God. Every time we discard a sin or a self-serving motive, every time we keep a trust or gain another glimpse of who we really are or speak truth, we are better able to build the kingdom of God. Every time we help someone else strengthen faith or resolve, we build the kingdom of God. In short, every small step we take to develop our God-given attributes of faith, knowledge, obedience, purity, integrity, identity, and courage makes us better able to build up the kingdom of God.

From the beginning, men and women of God, experiencing the perils unique to their days, have shown that it can be done. Mary and Eve were elected for difficult assignments. And so were we. They came to earth precisely when they were needed and, in Mary's case, even in the right lineage. So have we. They endured heartache and opposition. So must we. Neither one was perfect, but both lived up to their stewardships perfectly. And so must we. For being a latter-day man or woman of God is a sacred trust, and when the Lord trusts us, He can really use us.

I believe Mary and Eve are the two greatest women who have ever lived. But I also believe *we* are the greatest generation of men and women to have ever lived. This means we have more responsibility than any men and women have ever had. Now, the Lord doesn't ask us to be more than who we are. The reality of mortality is that our work never stops—not if we're serious about immortality. So I ask you, Will you join me in identifying *one thing* you can do to increase your faith and knowledge? If you will, your obedience and purity, integrity and sense of identity will also increase—with unflinching moral courage being the result. Latter-day men and women of God must have this courage if we are to be a light and a standard, if we are to open our mouths, if we are to be disturbers and annoyers of the adversary's kingdom, and if we are to build up the kingdom of God. We can do it. I know we can!

When I think of Mary and Eve, the words of Ruth to Naomi often run through my mind: "Whither thou goest, I will go; . . . thy people shall be my people, and thy God my God" (Ruth 1:16). I find myself wanting to say: Mary and Eve, whither thou goest, we will go. The path you have walked, we are trying to walk. The place you have gone is where we want to go, so that in a coming day we may all, men and women of God from every dispensation, be reunited and rejoice together over the miracle of this life and the miracle of eternal life.

Jesus *is* the Christ. He redeemed us from the Fall. There is no "other way nor name given . . . whereby [we] can be saved in the kingdom of God" (2 Nephi 31:21). And there is no greater joy and no greater work than helping the Lord with His work, because His work is our work.

May we have the courage to do what we were elected to do and what we agreed to do, so that every day, when we wake up, the Lord will say, "Terrific, they're awake again. Ready to help me build up my kingdom."

CHAPTER THREE

Are We Not All Mothers?

Motherhood is not what was left over after our
Father blessed His sons with the privilege of priesthood
ordination. It was the most ennobling endowment
He could give His daughters.

O NE SUMMER FOUR TEENAGE nieces and I shared a tense Sunday evening when we set out walking from a downtown hotel in a large U.S. city where we were visiting to a nearby chapel where I had been invited to speak at a fireside. I had walked that exact route many times before, but that evening as we left our hotel we suddenly found ourselves engulfed by an enormous crowd of rowdy, drunken parade-goers who were streaming out of the city toward the suburbs. Though police were everywhere, it was obviously no place for four teenage girls—or for their aunt, for that matter. But with the streets closed to traffic, and therefore no cabs available, we had no choice but to keep walking. Feeling no small amount of anxiety, I turned toward the girls, gathered them around me, and shouted over the din, "Stay right with me. Don't take your eyes off me." With that, I began to maneuver my way through the crush of humanity, constantly looking behind me to make sure the girls were right there. The *only* thing on my mind was my nieces' safety. There were moments when I truly feared we would not make it to the church in one piece. Drunken men with boa constrictors draped around their necks and adolescents brandishing weapons sometimes blocked our way. It was intimidating, to say the least.

Though our walk took twice as long as it should have, we finally made it to the chapel. But for ninety unnerving minutes, I better understood how mothers feel who forgo their own safety to protect their children. My siblings had entrusted me with their daughters, whom I dearly love, and I would have done just about anything to protect them and to lead them safely to our destination.

In a similar fashion, our Father has entrusted us, His daughters, with His children, and He has asked us not only to *love* them but to help *lead* them safely through the crush of mortal humanity and past the dangers of this world back home.

Loving and *leading*—these words summarize not only the all-consuming work of the Father and the Son, but the essence of the labor of women, for the work of latter-day women of God is to help the Lord with His work. How, then, may latter-day women of God best help the Lord with His work?

Prophets have repeatedly answered this question, as did the First Presidency six decades ago, when they called motherhood "the highest, holiest service . . . assumed by mankind" ("Message of the First Presidency to the Church," 761).

Have you ever wondered why prophets have taught the doctrine of motherhood—and it *is* doctrine—again and again, and without even the slightest variation? I have. I have thought long and hard about the work of women of God. And I have wrestled with what the doctrine of mother-hood means to *all* women. Because my life has unfolded in a manner far different than I had hoped or expected, the issue of motherhood has driven me to my knees, to the scriptures, to the temple, and to the teachings of prophets, seers, and revelators—all of which teach an ennobling doctrine regarding the most crucial role any woman can be asked or allowed to assume. It is a doctrine about which we must be clear if we hope to stand "steadfast and immovable" (Mosiah 5:15) and unflinching regarding the issues that swirl around the female gender.

For Satan has declared war on motherhood and on the family. He does everything he can to dishonor and devalue both womanhood and motherhood. This fact is more apparent with every passing day. He well knows that those who rock the cradle are perhaps in the best possible position to rock his diabolical earthly empire. He knows that none of us could progress without receiving bodies and experiencing our sec-ond estate. He understands that without mothers who are willing to bear children, our Father's plan would be completely frustrated. He knows that without righteous mothers loving and leading the rising generation, the kingdom of God will fail.

No wonder, then, if motherhood is divine and eternal and core to the nature of every woman, that Lucifer would do everything in his con-siderable power to demean and undermine everything about mother-hood, hoping to confuse women with worldly enticements or secular philosophies that appear more satisfying or dazzling or even more enlightening.

When we understand the magnitude of motherhood, it becomes

clear why prophets have been so protective of woman's most sacred and divinely appointed role. While *we* tend to equate motherhood solely with maternity and to, in effect, limit it to that definition, in the Lord's language the word *mother* has layers of meaning. Of all the words or titles they could have chosen to define her role and her essence, both God the Father and Adam called Eve "the mother of all living" (Moses 4:26)—and they did so *before* she ever bore a child. "And Adam called his wife's name Eve, because she was the mother of all living; for thus have I, the Lord God, called the first of all women, which are many" (Moses 4:26).

The Lord does nothing with a short-range view. Everything He does is for forever. Thus, like Eve, our motherhood began *before* we were born. Just as worthy men were foreordained to hold the priesthood in mortality (see Alma 13:2–4, 7–8), righteous women were endowed premortally with the privilege and responsibility of motherhood (see Spencer W. Kimball, "Role of Righteous Women," 102). Motherhood is more than bearing children, though it is certainly and definitely that. It is the essence of who we are as women. Motherhood defines our very identity, our divine stature and nature, and the unique traits, talents, and tendencies our Father gave us.

President Gordon B. Hinckley stated that "God planted within women something divine" (*Teachings of Gordon B. Hinckley,* 387). That something is the gift of and the gifts associated with motherhood. Elder Matthew Cowley of the Quorum of the Twelve taught that "men have to have something given to them [in mortality] to make them saviors of men, but not mothers, not women. [They] are born with an inherent right, an inherent authority, to be the saviors of human souls . . . and the regenerating force in the lives of God's children" (*Matthew Cowley Speaks*, 109).

Motherhood is not what was left over after our Father blessed His sons with the privilege of priesthood ordination. It was the most ennobling endowment He could give His daughters, a sacred trust that gave woman an unparalleled role in helping His children keep their second estate. As President J. Reuben Clark, Jr., declared, motherhood is "as divinely called, as eternally important in its place as the Priesthood itself" ("Our Wives and Our Mothers in the Eternal Plan," 801). And President Boyd K. Packer taught this: "The obligations of motherhood are never-ending. The addition of such duties as those which attend ordination to the priesthood would constitute an intrusion into, an interruption to, perhaps the avoidance of, that crucial contribution which only a mother can provide. The limitation of priesthood responsibilities to men is a tribute to the incomparable place of women in the plan of salvation. . . . Men and women have complementary, not competing, responsibilities. There is difference but not inequity. . . . In the woman's part, she is not equal to man; she is superior! She can do that which he can never do; not in all eternity can he do it" (*Things of the Soul,* Bookcraft, 172).

No wonder President Gordon B. Hinckley has declared that "mothers can do more than any other group" to reverse today's sobering social trends ("Walking in the Light of the Lord," 100).

There can be no question about how our Father feels about His daughters, whom He has charged with the principal care of His children. And there can be no question about why prophets ancient and modern have depended so heavily upon the influence of mothers, both in and outside the home, to help build the gospel kingdom.

Nevertheless, at times and in some circumstances, the words *mother* and *motherhood* have divided rather than united us. For the subject of motherhood is a very tender one, as it evokes some of our greatest joys and heartaches. This has been so from the very beginning. Eve was "glad" after the Fall, realizing she otherwise "never should have had seed" (Moses 5:11). And yet, imagine her anguish, sorrow, and suffering over Cain and her heartache about Abel. Some mothers experience pain because of the children they have borne; others feel pain because they do not have the privilege of bearing children here in mortality. About this Elder John A. Widtsoe was explicit: "Women who through no fault of their own cannot exercise the gift of motherhood directly, may do so vicariously" (*Priesthood and Church Government,* 85). And Elder Melvin J. Ballard stated: "God bless those mothers who are not yet permitted through no fault of their own to be mothers in very deed, but who are nevertheless mothers at heart" (*Sermons and Missionary Services of Melvin Joseph Ballard,* 206–7).

For reasons known to the Lord, some women are required to wait to have children. This delay and disappointment is not easy for any righteous woman. But the Lord's timetable for each of us does not negate or somehow change or cancel out our very nature. Some of us, then, must simply find other ways to mother. And all around us are those who need to be loved and led, nurtured and mentored. In other words, the spiritual rewards of mothering are available to all.

Eve set the pattern. In addition to bearing children, she mothered all of mankind when she made the most courageous decision any woman has ever made and with Adam opened the way for us to progress. She set an example of womanhood for men to respect and women to follow, modeling the characteristics with which we as women have been endowed: heroic faith, a keen sensitivity to the Spirit, an abhorrence of evil, and complete selflessness. Like the Savior, "who for the joy that was set before him endured the cross" (Hebrews 12:2), Eve, for the joy of helping initiate the human family, endured the Fall. She loved us enough to help lead us.

As daughters of our Heavenly Father, and as daughters of Eve, we are all mothers and we have always been mothers. And we each have the responsibility and the privilege to love and to help lead the rising generation. How will our young women learn to live as women of God unless they see what women of God look like—meaning what we wear, watch, and read; how we fill our time and our minds; how we face temptation and uncertainty; where we find true joy; and why modesty and femininity are hallmarks of righteous women? How will our young men, on the other hand, learn to value women of God if we don't show them the virtue of our virtues? If we don't show them what kind of women will help them find the greatest joy and fulfillment in their lives, who will? *One of the single most significant responsibilities for a latter-day woman of God—regardless of her personal circumstances—is to help love and lead the younger generation. If we don't mentor them, no one will. If we don't show them there is joy in living this way, where else can they possibly expect to see it!*

Every one of us has an overarching obligation to model righteous womanhood because our youth may not see it modeled anywhere else. Every sister in Relief Society, which is simply the most significant community of women on this side of the veil, is responsible to help our young women make a joyful transition into Relief Society. This means that our friendship with our young women must begin long before they turn eighteen. Every woman of God, regardless of our individual circumstances, can mother someone—beginning of course with the children in our own homes and families, but extending far beyond. Every woman of God can show by word and by deed that the work of women in the Lord's kingdom is magnificent and holy. How far will we go to rescue a child or rally a teenager to righteousness? For when we save a young man or a young woman, we may save generations. I repeat: *Every woman of God is a mother in Israel,* and our calling is to help love and help lead the rising generation through the dangerous streets of mortality.

Few of us will reach our potential without the nurturing of both the mother who bore us and the mothers who bear with us. I was thrilled not long ago to see one of my youth leaders for the first time in years. As a teenager who had absolutely no self-confidence, I always sidled up to this woman because she would inevitably put her arm around me and say, "You are just the best girl!" She showed that she loved me, so I was willing to let her lead me. How many young men and women are desperate for your love and leadership? Do we fully realize that our influence as mothers in Israel is irreplaceable and eternal?

When I was growing up, it was not uncommon for Mother to wake me in the middle of the night and say, "Sheri, take your pillow and go downstairs." I knew what that meant. We lived in Kansas, tornado country, and her words meant a tornado was coming. My immediate reaction was always fear. But then Mom would inevitably say, "Sheri, everything will be okay." Her words always calmed me, and even as a child I instinctively sensed that my mother was constantly looking out for me.

Later, as I grew older and began to enter musical competitions or participate on athletic teams, before big games or performances, again,

I would listen for my mother to say something like, "I just know you can do it. You'll be great."

It is interesting that today, decades later, when life seems particularly overwhelming or frightening or just downright scary, I call Mother and listen for her to say, "Sheri, everything will be okay." Because then I know it will. A mother's influence not only spans decades, it reaches into the eternities.

There are few women who exemplify this better than Lucy Mack Smith, mother of the Prophet Joseph. Long before her son had the experience in the Sacred Grove that commenced the Restoration, she was seeking to find the original gospel preached by the Savior as recorded in the scriptures. She went to one meeting with high hopes and recorded: "I went in expectation of obtaining that which alone could satisfy my soul—the bread of eternal life. When the minister commenced, I fixed my mind with breathless attention upon the spirit and matter of the discourse, but all was emptiness, vanity, vexation of spirit, and fell upon my heart like the chill, untimely blast upon the starting ear ripening in a summer sun. I was almost in total despair, and with a grieved and troubled spirit I returned home, saying in my heart, there is not on earth the religion which I seek. I must again turn to my Bible, take Jesus and his disciples for an example."

Later, when she nearly died of tuberculosis, she wrote, "I covenanted with God that if he would let me live, I would endeavor to get that religion that would enable me to serve him right, whether it was in the Bible or wherever it might be found, even if it was to be obtained from heaven by prayer and faith" (*History of Joseph Smith by His Mother*, 48–50).

Surely Lucy Mack's fundamental faith, searching, and spiritual sensitivity paved the way for all that would happen to her sons Joseph and Hyrum. Her influence has clearly reached into the eternities.

After the horrifying events of September 11, 2001, U.S. First Lady Laura Bush was asked to recount what she did during those initial minutes after she heard about the terrorist attack. "I called my children immediately to reassure them," she said, adding, "and then I called my own mother, just for the comfort of her voice" ("Laura Bush, Comforter in Chief," from WashingtonPost.com, 21 September 2001).

Terrorist activities and ongoing armed conflicts underscore the fact that we live in a world of uncertainty and unmitigated evil. Never has there been a greater need for righteous mothers—mothers who bless their children with a sense of safety, security, and confidence about the future, mothers who teach their children where to find peace and truth and that the power of Jesus Christ is always stronger than the power of the adversary.

Recently one of my sisters found an old notebook containing the minutes of a home Primary our mother held in 1957 because there was only one Primary-age child in our little branch—a four-year-old girl. Me. Week after week, Mother prepared a lesson and taught a song. Usually there was one visitor: my two-year-old brother. Page after page records the consistent efforts of a young mother to teach her children the gospel.

That notebook has caused me to reflect yet again on the countless ways Mother helped set the course for my life. For what a mother teaches a child doesn't get erased.

Every time we build the faith or reinforce the nobility of a young woman or man, every time we love or lead anyone even one small step along the path, we are true to our endowment and calling and inherent nature as mothers. No woman who understands the gospel would ever think that any other work is more important or would ever say, "I am *just* a mother," for mothers heal the souls of men.

I invite every woman to look around. Who needs you and your influence? Who needs your healing, nurturing touch? Who needs someone to understand them and to believe in them? Who needs to hear you say, "I know things are going to be all right," or, "I just know you can do it."

If we really want to make a difference, it will happen as we mother those we have borne and those we are willing to bear with. If we will stay right with our youth—meaning, if we will *love* them—in most cases, they will stay right with us, meaning, they will let us *lead* them. And in the process we will find joy, for as Elder John A. Widtsoe declared, "Where women choose to magnify their motherhood, either direct or vicarious, progress and happiness is the sure result" (*Priesthood and Church Government*, 90).

As mothers in Israel, we *are* the Lord's secret weapon. Our influence comes from a divine endowment that has been in place from the beginning. In the premortal world, when our Father described our role, I wonder if we didn't stand in wide-eyed wonder that He would bless us with a sacred trust so central to His plan and that He would endow us with gifts so vital to the loving and leading of His children. I wonder if we shouted for joy (see Job 38:7) at least in part because of the ennobling stature He gave us in His kingdom. The world won't tell you that, but the Spirit will.

We just cannot let the Lord down. And if the day comes when Latter-day Saint women are the only women on earth who find nobility and divinity in motherhood, so be it. For *mother* is the word that will define a righteous woman made perfect in the highest degree of the celestial kingdom, a woman who has qualified for eternal increase in posterity, wisdom, joy, and influence.

I know without question or reservation that these doctrines about the divine role of women are true, and that when understood they bring peace and purpose to all women. The challenge of all latter-day women of God is to rise to the responsibility of being mothers in these perilous times, though doing so may test the last ounce of our endurance and courage and faith. Our challenge is to stand steadfast and immovable and unflinching as mothers in Israel and women of God. Our Father and His Only Begotten Son have given us a sacred stewardship and a holy crown in Their kingdom. May we rejoice in it. And may we be worthy of Their trust.

CHAPTER FOUR

It Is Not Good for Man or Woman to Be Alone

*When women understand and fully respect the fact
that the Church is governed by the power of the priesthood,
and when priesthood leaders in turn acknowledge the unique contribution
of women, the work can move forward to bless countless people.*

FOR FIVE YEARS I HAD THE PRIVILEGE of serving with Relief Society sisters and priesthood leaders from Africa to the Amazon. These experiences with spectacularly good men and women the world over reinforced for me the importance of a fundamental gospel and eternal principle that influences what takes place in literally every imaginable setting.

To explain what I am referring to, let me describe an experience I had one summer when I severely injured a shoulder and lost the use of an arm for weeks. Before that time—and isn't this so true in like situations—I hadn't realized how much one arm depends upon the other for balance, or how much less I could lift with one arm than two, or that there were some things I simply couldn't do at all. This disability not only renewed my respect for those who deal so well with a physical limitation of any kind, but helped me realize how much more two arms working together can do than one arm going it alone.

This really shouldn't be a surprise, however. For two are usually better than one (see Ecclesiastes 4:9), as our Father confirmed when He declared that "it was not good that the man should be alone" (Moses 3:18; see also Abraham 5:14) and made a help meet for Adam—someone with distinct gifts who would give him balance, someone who would help him shoulder and lift the burdens of mortality, and someone who would bring out the best in him and enable him to do things he couldn't do alone. For "neither is the man without the woman, neither the woman without the man, in the Lord" (1 Corinthians 11:11).

Satan understands the power and potential of men and women united in righteousness. He is still stinging from his banishment into eternal exile after Michael led the hosts of heaven, comprised of valiant men and women united in the cause of Christ, against him. Lucifer seems particularly determined to devour marriages and families, because their demise threatens to destabilize not only mortal society but the salvation of all involved and the vitality of the Lord's kingdom itself. Thus, from time immemorial Satan has attempted to confuse us about our stewardships and distinctive natures as men and women. He bombards us with bizarre messages about gender, marriage, family, and essentially every male-female relationship. He would have us believe men and women are so alike that our unique gifts are not necessary, or so different that we can never hope to understand each other. But neither of these messages is true.

Our Father knew exactly what He was doing when He created us. He made us enough alike to love, value, and be attracted to each other, but enough different that we would complement each other and would in fact need to unite our strengths and weaknesses to create a whole. Neither man nor woman is perfect or complete without the other. Thus, no marriage or family, no ward or stake is likely to reach its full potential until husbands and wives, mothers and fathers, men and women work together in unity of purpose, respecting and relying upon each other's strengths.

These truths about the divinely appointed stewardships of men and women are largely (and increasingly) lost on the world today. You will not find them in very many movies or television sitcoms; you will not find them represented in many contemporary novels; and sadly, you will not even find them in some homes or wards. But they are not lost to the Lord, who has given us "a pattern in all things, that [we] may not be deceived" (D&C 52:14). The Lord's pattern for couples and in large measure men and women serving together in His kingdom was established by our first parents. *Together* Adam and Eve labored, mourned, were obedient, had children, taught their posterity the gospel, felt joy, called upon the name of the Lord, "heard the voice of the Lord," blessed the name of God, endured the wilderness, and dedicated themselves to God. Repeatedly the scriptures about Adam and Eve refer to the pronoun *they* (see Moses 5:1, 4, 12, 27; 2 Nephi 2:20).

Neither Adam with his priesthood nor Eve with her motherhood could bring about the Fall alone. Their unique roles were interconnected. They counseled with and consoled one another, learned and grew together, lifted burdens neither could have lifted alone, and then faced the wilderness, with all of its uncertainty, together. This is the Lord's pattern for righteous men and women.

Now, some of us encounter life circumstances that are less than ideal. I understand this in a very personal way. For decades I have pleaded with the Lord for the privilege of marrying and having a family. To this point, those prayers have not been answered in the way I have asked them to be. And yet, I cannot deny (and would never wish to do so) that our understanding and testimony of this divine pattern is absolutely imperative, perhaps more so today than ever before. Our understanding of this divine pattern affects our attitudes about gender, marriage, and family. It affects our ability to help build up the kingdom. It even affects our ability ultimately to receive eternal life.

In this most unusual and confusing era in which we live, some will try to convince us as women that because we are not ordained to hold the priesthood we have somehow been shortchanged. They are, very simply, either misguided or flat-out wrong, and they do not understand the gospel of Jesus Christ. They do not understand how God our Father feels about and regards His daughters; they do not understand the phenomenal respect that Jesus Christ demonstrated for women during mortality and that His gospel makes manifest. The blessings of the priesthood are available equally to *every* righteous man and woman. We may *all* receive the Holy Ghost, obtain personal revelation, and be endowed in the temple, from which we emerge "armed" with power (see D&C 109:22). The power of the priesthood heals, protects, and inoculates all of the righteous against the powers of darkness. Most significantly, the fulness of the priesthood contained in the highest ordinances of the house of the Lord can be received only by a man and woman together (see D&C 131:1–4; 132:19–20). Said President Harold B. Lee: "Pure womanhood plus priesthood means exaltation. But womanhood without priesthood, or priesthood without pure womanhood doesn't spell exaltation" (*Teachings of Harold B. Lee*, 292).

Many leaders through the ages have further clarified this doctrine. President Joseph Fielding Smith taught that "there is no exaltation in the kingdom of God without the fullness of the priesthood, and every man who receives the Melchizedek Priesthood does so with an oath and a covenant that he shall be exalted. . . . [But] the blessings of the priesthood are not confined to men alone. These blessings are also poured out upon our wives and daughters and upon all the faithful women of the Church. . . . The Lord offers to his daughters every spiritual gift and blessing that can be obtained by his sons" ("Magnifying Our Callings in the Priesthood," 66). And Elder James E. Talmage explained as follows: "It is not given to women to exercise the authority of the Priesthood independently; nevertheless, in the sacred endowments associated with the ordinances pertaining to the House of the Lord, woman shares with man the blessings of the Priesthood. When the frailties and imperfections of mortality are left behind, in the glorified state of the blessed hereafter, husband and wife will administer in their respective stations, . . . and co-operating to the full in the government of their family kingdom" ("Eternity of Sex," 602–3).

More recently, President Spencer W. Kimball taught that the roles and assignments of men and women differ, with "women being given many tremendous responsibilities of motherhood and sisterhood and men being given the tremendous responsibilities of fatherhood and the priesthood—but the man is not without the woman nor the woman without the man. . . . Remember, in the world before we came here, faithful women were given certain assignments while faithful men were foreordained to certain priesthood tasks. While we do not now remember the particulars, this does not alter the glorious reality of what we once agreed to. . . . This leaves much to be done by way of parallel personal development—for both men and women" ("Role of Righteous Women," 102).

Very simply, we as women are not diminished by priesthood power, we are magnified by it. I know this is true, for I have experienced it again and again. Those who remain troubled by this issue, or who are simply seeking for further knowledge and understanding, may wish to spend more time in the temple and listen carefully to what is taught. Watch for patterns and sequences. In particular, listen to the phrases and promises associated with the word *power*, all while reflecting on that power and what it is and means. In the House of the Lord, where men and women alike partake of sacred, binding, exalting ordinances, it becomes increasingly clear why this issue of priesthood and women is not an issue at all.

I repeat, we as women are not diminished by priesthood power, we are magnified by it.

Our husbands, the other men in our families, and the men with whom we serve need and deserve the support only we can give. We have an inner spiritual strength—divinely endowed, I believe—that in many instances even sets us apart. Said President James E. Faust to the women of the Church: "As daughters of God, you cannot imagine the divine potential within each of you. Surely the secret citadel of women's inner strength is spirituality. In this you equal and even surpass men, as you do in faith, morality, and commitment when truly converted to the gospel. You have 'more trust in the Lord [and] more hope in his word.' (*Hymns*, no. 131.) This inner spiritual sense seems to give you a certain resilience to cope with sorrow, trouble, and uncertainty" ("What It Means to Be a Daughter of God," 101). As latter-day women of God, we simply must not abdicate our spiritual responsibility. Our faith will preach compelling sermons to our companions and colleagues in the work of the Lord. No amount of time in front of the mirror will make us as attractive as will having the Holy Ghost with us. Our charge is to bless our families and friends and the Church as only a woman of God can—with virtue, faith, integrity, and constant compassion.

For men, the privilege of being ordained to hold the priesthood is a holy and sacred privilege and an equally grand and imposing responsibility, but not a license to dominate or intimidate. My hope is that latter-day men of God would be unfailingly worthy to exercise this godly power, which is given to men to enable them to render service. From my point of view and from my experience, a man is never more magnificent than when he is guided by the Spirit to honor and act within the bounds of the priesthood he holds.

When a man chooses to marry a virtuous woman who can hear the voice of the Lord, she will bless his life every day of his life. Consider Eve. She was the first to see that the fruit of the tree was good, and after partaking, she "gave unto her husband . . . , and he did eat" (Moses 4:12). Were it not for Eve, our progression would have ceased. Elder Dallin H. Oaks taught that Eve's "act, whatever its nature, was formally a transgression but eternally a glorious necessity to open the doorway toward eternal life. Adam showed his wisdom by doing the same. And thus Eve and 'Adam fell that men might be.' (2 Nephi 2:25.)" ("Great Plan of Happiness," 73).

Men preside at home and in the Church. As the Proclamation on the Family declares with reference to the most fundamental unit of society, "By divine design, fathers are to preside over their families in love and righteousness and are responsible to provide the necessities of life and protection for their families." But may I suggest that a wise man is

one who is humble enough to listen to and learn from the women in his
life. Women will provide insight, balance, perspective, and a unique
kind of wisdom. And when challenges come, men will see how resilient
a woman committed to God the Father and Jesus Christ is.

This divine pattern for men and women that strengthens marriages
and families also fortifies the Church. For the Church cannot achieve
the full measure of its creation unless both faithful men who bear the
priesthood and righteous women who understand the source of priesthood power and rejoice in serving under the direction of those holding
the priesthood work together. Time and again I have experienced this
joy.

I think of a meeting in Brazil where I had a translator who was
unsure of her ability to convert my English into Portuguese. But as it
turned out, she and I communicated that evening with ease. After the
meeting I learned one of the reasons why. I found that not only had the
General Authority who presided been literally on the edge of his seat
behind us the entire meeting, prompting the translator when necessary,
but he had also assigned another priesthood leader to pray for both of
us throughout the meeting.

That General Authority created a safety net of support so that I
could fulfill the assignment *he* had given me. On another occasion, that
same General Authority, again presiding at a training meeting of Relief
Society and priesthood leaders in northeastern Brazil, interrupted my
presentation several times throughout the evening to reaffirm from his
point of view what I was teaching and to endorse what I had taught.

On another occasion, Sister Sharon Larsen and I had the privilege
of serving under the direction of a General Authority on a trip throughout southeast Asia. Every day we traveled to a new country with its own

unique customs and cultures, and every day we had the privilege of meeting new leaders and members of the Church. It was a particular joy to serve under this priesthood leader's direction. He made us feel like vital members of his team. When auxiliary and priesthood leaders asked difficult questions, he often called upon one of us to respond, implying that we knew the answers just as he did. He treated us as though he just assumed we understood the doctrine, understood Church policies, understood when to speak and when to stop speaking. He made us feel as though he was counting on our contribution. We loved serving under his direction. There was no question about who was presiding. But there was a joyful kind of synergy that came from serving under this dynamic but respectful leader.

I served as a stake Relief Society president under a stake president who treated me with great respect. One example is representative of countless others I had with him: One day I went to him with a concern I had detected among the auxiliary leaders in the stake. He responded by inviting me to join him in presenting a message on the topic at the next stake bishops' meeting. He told me generally what he wished for me to cover and outlined what he in turn would teach.

At the appointed hour I arrived at the stake offices and waited outside the high council room, where the meeting was already in progress. A few minutes later, the stake executive secretary opened the door and invited me to come in. The instant I stepped across the threshold, the stake president rose to his feet, and the other men in the room followed suit. This simple gesture took me by surprise, and my eyes began to fill with tears. The stake president said, "Sister Dew, we've saved a seat for you up here by the presidency. Please join us." Then he told the bishops why he had invited me and asked them to pay close attention to what I had to say. When I had concluded, he stood and said, simply, "I want to endorse everything Sister Dew has taught you. If you take her words seriously and act upon them, it will make a difference for the women and children in your wards."

How do you think I felt about serving under the direction of this inspired leader? I would have moved heaven and earth to do what he asked me to do, because I felt that he sincerely valued not only my contribution but the contributions of all the women in the stake.

When women understand and fully respect the fact that the Church is governed by the power of the priesthood, and when priesthood leaders in turn acknowledge the unique contribution of women, the work can move forward to bless countless people. This can happen in every ward and stake and, first and foremost, in every home when egos are laid aside, pretenses are dropped, and we simply learn to rejoice in each other's unique talents and gifts.

The circle of support derived from righteous men and women serving together has no end, because there is no end to the good works of righteous men and women who respect each other and who thrust in their sickles and reap, side by side, in the Lord's vineyard. If we are going to build families unto the Lord, and if we are going to build the kingdom of God, we as men and women of God must build each other. There is no challenge—in our families, with activation or retention, with missionary work, or even with the onslaught of evils and ills that seems to characterize today's world—that we can't face and solve when we counsel together in councils and help each other lift the load. It is simply not intended for any of us to try to lift the load alone.

There is much to learn from the Lord's pattern for men and women. It is worth pondering the scriptural accounts of Adam and Eve to better

understand what the Lord wants us to learn about strengthening marriages, families, and wards and stakes. The devastating events of
September 11, 2001, in the United States seemed to signal even more
difficult days ahead, which is proving to be true. But we are living in
days that will be filled with confidence and courage if we, as men and
women, unite in righteousness as never before. There is no limit to what
we may accomplish if we will work together, equally yoked, under the
guidance of the priesthood.

Our Father's patterns help us avoid deception. Hence the wisdom
in looking to the Lord and not to the world for our ideas and our ideals
about men and women. Hence the wisdom in building our families and
the kingdom together, for it is simply not good for man or woman to be
alone. If we will lift each other, together we will be able to lift the beautiful burdens of mortality and have glory added upon our heads forever
(see Abraham 3:26). The Lord simply must have righteous men and
righteous women working together to build up His kingdom.

Standing Tall and Standing Together

❖

CHAPTER FIVE

A Glimpse at Faith, Hope, and Charity

When we really believe in Jesus Christ—
meaning that He will overrule for our good and
that He knows who we are—that kind of faith naturally
creates a feeling of hope and optimism.

SERMONS ON THE SUBJECT OF FAITH, hope, and charity are plentiful. Because these principles are so fundamental to our understanding of the gospel of Jesus Christ and so central to our personal conversion and to our ability to live as sons and daughters of Christ, scarcely a general conference passes without our hearing more messages on these triplet doctrines and their interrelationship with each other.

Certainly the most enduring sermon on faith, hope, and charity—and the one most quoted in all the others—is that of the prophet Mormon recorded by his son in Moroni 7. I have perhaps studied and reflected on and prayed about this particular chapter of scripture as much as any other, prompted, at least in part, by twenty-five years of service in various capacities in the Relief Society, whose motto, "Charity

Never Faileth," is quoted there (Moroni 7:46). I have underlined the relevant verses, cross-referenced them with many others, and written copious notes in the margins of my scriptures about the essential relationship of these fundamental gospel principles.

In recent months, however, I have had cause to reflect again on these principles, because it dawned on me one day that I had observed what is perhaps their perfect union in the life of someone I had known for many years. President Gordon B. Hinckley has stated, after all, that the "most persuasive gospel tract is the exemplary life of a faithful Latter-day Saint" (*Teachings of Gordon B. Hinckley,* 182). And in the life of his dear wife, Sister Marjorie P. Hinckley, who passed away on April 6, 2004, those who knew her witnessed an embodiment, a real-life glimpse of what happens when the virtues of faith, hope, and charity come together in the life of a man or woman.

When I learned that Sister Hinckley had slipped through the veil, I had a flood of emotions. But through my tears I felt a sweet jubilation. I couldn't help but think, She did it! She did what she came here to do. And she did it magnificently. For everywhere she went, Marjorie Hinckley left *everyone* she met better and happier and more confident than she found them. It is as a family friend said after her parting, "She is one of those rare people who looked better and better the closer you got."

Ten years ago I set out to study the life of President Gordon B. Hinckley. But it quickly became apparent that it wasn't possible to study his life without studying hers, because they were hand in glove. A matched set. And thus began one of the most delightful privileges and learning experiences of my life.

Sister Hinckley was bright and quick and real. There were never any pretenses with her—nothing was put on for show. She had an unbelievable sense of humor. And curiously, I always left her presence feeling better about myself. I quickly saw that she was a perpetual transfusion of good cheer for her husband. But even more, everyone who knew her well said she had the same effect on them. One granddaughter said it this way: "I never talk with Grandma that I don't feel a surge of energy. If she thinks I can do something, then I can."

Marjorie Hinckley had the same effect on me, and for years I tried to put my finger on exactly what it was that made her so irresistible and that made everyone who knew her clamor to be in her presence. Those who knew her best would speak of her charm and warmth and good humor. They said she was the most nonjudgmental, supportive, encouraging, optimistic person they had ever met. They insisted that if they could package her unique brand of optimism and joy, they could make a fortune and change the world in the process. But none of those descriptors, as glowing as they are, ever seemed to really do her justice. Then, not long before she passed away, while I was studying yet again Moroni's description of his father's discourse on faith, hope, and charity, it dawned on me—Marjorie Hinckley *was* faith, hope, and charity personified.

Her optimism and hope sprang from her deep faith in Jesus Christ. And the natural by-product of hope borne of faith is charity, or the ability to truly care about others more than about yourself.

As I read Moroni 7, I could see her name in every verse, especially these: "And [Marjorie Hinckley] suffereth long, and is kind, and envieth not, and is not puffed up, seeketh not her own, is not easily provoked, thinketh no evil, and rejoiceth not in iniquity but rejoiceth in the truth, beareth all things, believeth all things, hopeth all things, endureth all things. Wherefore, . . . if ye have not charity, ye are nothing, for charity never faileth" (Moroni 7:45–46).

That explained it. What *everyone* felt in her presence was the pure love of Christ, the love the Father bestows upon all "who are true followers of his Son, Jesus Christ" (Moroni 7:48). It was the pure love of Christ that allowed her to stop worrying about how the world saw and treated her, and left her free to focus her attention on others. It was the pure love of Christ that allowed her to rejoice in the accomplishments of others without feeling jealous or intimidated; to focus intently on others rather than worry how she was being viewed. It was the pure love of Christ that, over time, made her oblivious to the enticements of the world. It was because she was filled with the pure love of Christ that she never failed to have the impact on others that she had. And the results were stunning.

Sister Hinckley simply *chose* to see the best in every situation. She loved people and believed in them. According to Marjorie Hinckley, everyone was good. She was either unable or unwilling to see the negative in others. Her son Dick said she put Will Rogers to shame.

When the children were younger and she traveled less frequently with her husband, she didn't moan about his absences. She would often say to the children, "Oh, good, your father is gone. Let's order pizza"—something they did not indulge in otherwise. "Mother put no pressure on Dad," her daughter Virginia reflected later. "He was free to do what he had been asked to do, without worrying that she was secretly resenting his time away. Mother made us feel it was a privilege for our father to serve the Lord."

When Kathy lived in Hawaii and lamented missing the fruit that grew in her parents' yard, her mother wrote: "Don't grieve over the cherries. Enjoy the pineapple and mangoes." It was vintage Marjorie Hinckley. There was never a need to focus on what she didn't have.

Here are some of the things she said again and again:

"Make life an adventure."

"Are there not days when you are simply overwhelmed by the blessings of the Lord?"

"The only way to get through life is to laugh your way through it."

"When you see what's happening in this Church, it's thrilling to get up every morning."

And, "Life is more than I ever imagined it would be."

As much as Marjorie Hinckley loved and believed in others, she believed in no one more than her husband. A year after President Hinckley's ordination as President of the Church, she said in a regional conference: "He has always been a wonderful man, but there is something special about him now. The mantle is upon him, and I try to remember that when he leaves his ties draped over the sofa. I try to remember that he isn't perfect, just almost perfect. I am grateful to share his life with him."

With her husband, Sister Hinckley traveled far and wide to speak to audiences large and small, tracted with missionaries in faraway places, and called parents upon her return to the States to give them a firsthand account of their son or daughter. Together she and her husband walked the streets of Hong Kong and London, met in steamy rooms with small groups of Saints, slept in dilapidated hotels, and rode overnight trains and planes and steamships to reach the Saints in far-flung areas.

Days on the road with her husband were packed from dawn to way past dusk. But the fatigue was always worth it because, as she explained,

"When you get where you're going and meet the people, it's wonderful because *they* are wonderful."

Sometimes the travel seemed like a marathon. One letter home described a typical traveling schedule with her husband: "Sunday was a full day. We started with a serviceman's conference at 8:00 A.M. Then a conference with all the Chinese members at 10:00 A.M. Said good-bye to Taiwan and all our friends and flew to Okinawa and got there 30 minutes late for a meeting with the Japanese members at 7:30 P.M. And then rushed across the island for a serviceman's conference at 8:30 P.M. Monday morning we started the routine all over again."

A mission president's wife who traveled with the Hinckleys remembered: "Sister Hinckley was a trooper. It was sticky hot in the Philippines, but she went everywhere, traveled when she was exhausted, and kept us laughing. One day we were trying to cross the street in typhoon-like weather when Sister Hinckley tripped on a curb and went down. But she popped back up as though nothing had happened and marched straight on."

During a luncheon where she learned about the accomplishments of Susa Young Gates, she turned to Camilla Kimball and said, "It makes me wonder what I am doing with my life." "You are running to and from," Sister Kimball quipped. Marjorie concluded, "I *am* running to and from and shiver to think that someday I will have to account for the time spent."

And yet, she was even cheerful about always having more to do than time in which to do it. "Life gets that way when you belong to the true Church," she said.

Her native cheerfulness made her like an elixir to family, friends, and Church members everywhere. Women in particular, from small branches in Korea to the Marriott Center at BYU, soaked up everything she had to say. Her grandchildren hung on every word, as in this note to a granddaughter: "We are so proud to be your grandparents. I sometimes wonder if you are truly real. My challenge is to be worthy of you." She was even good-humored about her advancing age: "Oh, to be seventy again."

Her humor often provided just the right touch. When the weight of the world was pressing in upon her husband, she seemed to know how to lighten his load. When she came home one afternoon to find him working at his desk, having been evicted from his office so repairs could be made, she laughed out loud and asked if it was really necessary for him to wear his tie at home. He replied that no, he didn't have to, but his speech into the dictaphone was more dignified when he did. But then he couldn't resist chuckling.

She even learned to adjust to her husband's tendency to make last-minute travel arrangements. One incident is family legend. The night before a trip to South America, when she asked if she should plan to go with him, he responded, "Can't we decide that in the morning?"

And when President Hinckley would call on her to speak without warning, she took it in stride, often kidding him from the pulpit: "I can tell you why my husband called on me," she would say to the congregation. "It's because he's still figuring out what he wants to say, and I'm supposed to stall."

Through it all, she found joy in the journey, side by side with her husband. So much so that on their fifty-ninth anniversary she said, "It has been fifty-nine years of heaven on earth."

It is safe to say that it was fifty-nine years of heaven on earth, at least in part, because of the splendid coming together of faith, hope, and charity in her life, which she then shared with everyone who came within her sphere of influence, beginning with her husband and children.

Marjorie Hinckley demonstrated for us all, without fanfare or a desire to attract anyone's attention, what happens when faith, hope, and charity come together in a man or woman's life. For when we really believe in Jesus Christ—meaning we believe that He will overrule for our good and that He knows who we are and where we are and what we need—that kind of faith naturally creates a feeling of hope and optimism. We can hope not just for a better world somewhere out in the great beyond, but for a better world here and now. We can have hope for our lives and our families' lives. We can have hope that we definitely can endure and do what we have been called upon to do here. With that kind of hope and faith, it's impossible not to start looking outward instead of inward, and to think of others more than ourselves. And that is when pure charity begins to develop and mature. Perhaps the clearest indication that an endowment of the pure love of Christ is growing inside us is if our view increasingly turns outward rather than being so focused on ourselves.

Faith, hope, and charity are simply and fundamentally crucial to our conversion and to our eventual exaltation.

In President Hinckley's first general conference address, in April 1958, he said that "all of us are largely the product of the lives [that] touch [ours]" (in *Conference Report,* April 1958, 125). I am deeply grateful for the privilege of knowing a woman whose life has touched so many of us and from whom we have learned much: That living the gospel is the only way to be happy, and that being happy is a choice. That it is possible for a woman to be intensely supportive of her husband while continuing to grow herself. That when a righteous man and woman commit to each other completely, the bond is impenetrable and eternal. That an unpretentious woman filled with the pure love of Christ and devoted to Him can move about the entire earth and leave everyone she meets better than she found him or her. That a testimony of Jesus Christ is what undergirds it all. And that it really *is* possible, in the latter part of the latter days, to do what we came here to do, and to do it with joy.

Marjorie Pay Hinckley was not a perfect woman and would shudder at the thought of being represented as such. But she *was* proof positive that faith, hope, and charity are not just high-sounding principles that make for a great talk, but are core principles that can change our lives forever. I will be grateful the rest of my life for the privilege of knowing and loving and learning from this magnificent woman, who has given us a glimpse of what faith, hope, and charity look like in the life of someone willing to turn herself over to the Lord.

CHAPTER SIX

God Wants a Powerful People

*If God wants a powerful people who can withstand the
wiles of the devil (and He does), and if we were born to lead in these latter
days (and we were), then we need to understand how God makes His power
available to us, and how we gain access to that power.*

TWO CHRISTMASES AGO, I went out to my car one evening to find the passenger window smashed and my briefcase stolen with everything in it—money, credit cards, all of my I.D. (including the passport that had taken me to 50 countries), and several folders of irreplaceable documents. I was beside myself. The inconvenience coupled with the loss promised to make the next few days miserable, unless I could somehow retrieve some of the items. Hoping the thieves had stolen the money and discarded everything else, a friend and I spent all night prowling through area dumpsters, hoping to find something. Anything. But nothing. Amidst constant prayers that somehow a miracle would unfold, I nonetheless began the next day the tedious process of trying to replace or duplicate the contents. Suffice it to say, the whole process was a giant pain.

Then, unexpectedly, two mornings later, my phone rang at 3:00 A.M. It was a Church operator. "Sister Dew, did you lose a briefcase?" "Yes," I answered. "I have a man on the line who says he found it in a dumpster behind a bar. Been to any bars lately, Sister Dew?" Laughing at her own joke, she connected me with this man whose pickup, as it turned out, had been robbed that night and who had been going through dumpsters. In one he had found a briefcase. *My* briefcase. When I asked how he had tracked me down, he replied, "When I looked inside the briefcase and saw that 'Mormon Recommendation,' I knew this must be important." He was of course referring to my temple recommend. He had then called the Church number, where the operator on duty knew how to reach me.

The phrase "Mormon recommendation" instantly triggered a reminder of Mormon's tender words to his son Moroni: "I *recommend* thee unto God, and I trust in Christ that thou wilt be saved" (Moroni 9:22; emphasis added). I have often pondered what it would mean to be recommended to God. And yet, in essence, every time we qualify for a temple recommend, our priesthood leaders *are* doing just that.

But on this subject of recommendation there is another dimension to consider. God our Father and His Son Jesus Christ, with Their perfect foreknowledge and boundless wisdom, already recommended every one of us to fill our mortal probation during the most decisive period in the history of the world. We are here now because we were *elected* to be here now (see 1 Peter 1:2).

This is not new news. We have been told countless times that we comprise chosen generations, reserved for the latter part of the latter days. As a young Laurel attending the first (and perhaps only) Churchwide Laurel conference in the fall of 1970, I remember sitting in the Wilkinson Center Ballroom at BYU and hearing President Harold B. Lee tell us we were the finest generation the Church had ever seen, and that if we had any reservations about the truthfulness of the gospel, we should lean on his testimony until our own testimonies were strong.

Repeatedly President Gordon B. Hinckley has told the youth and young adults of the Church that they are "the best generation we have ever had" ("An Ensign to the Nations, a Light to the World," 84). And that trend won't stop. Clearly, our Father held in reserve His most noble sons and daughters for the latter part of the latter days (see George Q. Cannon, *Gospel Truth*, 18). It's akin to being chosen to run the last leg of a relay, where the coach always positions his strongest runner.

We were recommended to help run the last leg of the relay that began with Adam and Eve because our premortal spiritual valor indicated we would have the courage and the determination to face the world at its worst, to do combat with the evil one during his heyday, and in spite of it all to be fearless in building up the kingdom of God.

We simply *must* understand this, because *we were born to lead.* By virtue of who we are, the covenants we have made, and the fact that we are here now in the conclusive and pivotal eleventh hour, *we were born to lead.* As mothers and fathers, because nowhere is righteous leadership more crucial than in the family. As priesthood and auxiliary leaders. As heads of communities, companies, and even nations. As men and women willing to "stand as witnesses of God at *all times* and in *all things,* and in *all places*" (Mosiah 18:9)—because that's what a true leader does. *We were born to lead.* And in the words of Isaiah, *we were born for glory* (see Isaiah 62:2–3).

Now, the glorious but sobering truth is that, in spite of our aeons of premortal preparation, the days ahead will at times "wrench [our] very heart strings," as the Prophet Joseph told the Twelve (as quoted by John Taylor in *Journal of Discourses*, 24:197). If we've hoped to live out our lives passively, comfortably, let me burst that little bubble once and for all. Now, please, *do not* misunderstand me: This is a magnificent time to live! It is a time, said President Spencer W. Kimball, when our influence can be "tenfold what it might be in more tranquil times" ("Privileges and Responsibilities of Sisters," 103). The strongest runner *wants* to run the last leg of the relay. We may very well have volunteered for this duty.

But the last days are not for the faint of heart or the spiritually out-of-shape. There will be days when we feel defeated, exhausted, and plain old beat up by life's whiplash. People we love will disappoint us— and we will disappoint them. We'll probably struggle with some kind of mortal appetite. Some days it will feel as though the veil between heaven and earth is made of reinforced concrete. And we may even face a crisis of faith. In fact, we can count on trials that test our testimony and our faith.

Lest I leave a negative impression about our lives and our future, let me hastily add that I am nothing if not optimistic about our time here in our mortal probation. Everything about our lives is an indicator of our Father's remarkable respect, that He *recommended* us for now, when the stakes are so high, when His kingdom is being established once and for all, never again to be taken from the earth. He chose us for the last leg of the relay when He needs His strongest runners.

The simple fact is that our Father did not recommend Eve or Moses or Nephi or countless other magnificent exemplars for *this* dispensation. He *recommended* you and me. Do you think God would have left the last days to chance by sending men and women He couldn't count on? A common theme of patriarchal blessings given to our youth these days is that they were sent now because our Father's most trustworthy children would be needed in the final, decisive battle for righteousness. That is who our youth are, and it is who they have always been.

So, how will we live up to our Father's *recommendation?* Happily, though we must each walk through life on our own, we don't have to do it alone. Here are four principles to consider:

• God wants a powerful people.

• He gives His power to those who are faithful.

• Therefore, we have a sacred obligation to seek after the power of God and then to use that power as He directs.

• When we have the power of God with us, nothing is impossible.

I repeat, God wants a powerful people. Ammon taught that "a man may have great *power* given him from God" (Mosiah 8:16), and Nephi prophesied that we of the latter days would be "armed with . . . the *power* of God in great glory" (1 Nephi 14:14).

There are many evidences that God wants a powerful people. This is one reason that at baptism we become eligible to receive the gift of the Holy Ghost and the privilege of constant access to the third member of the Godhead.

This is one reason that twelve-year-old boys may be ordained to the Aaronic Priesthood, which holds "the key of the ministering of angels" (D&C 84:26).

This is one reason every worthy adult may go to the temple, from which he or she emerges surrounded and protected by God's power (see D&C 109:22).

God wants a powerful people. No one better understands that Satan is real and that he has power. No one better understands that none of us are smart or resilient enough to spar with Satan and survive spiritually. He is a snake.

A few years ago, while visiting the Philippines with its lush green countryside and humid, tropical climate, I asked a Filipino mission president if there were many snakes in his country. His answer was classic: "Where der is grass, der is snake." Meaning, the disgusting reptiles were everywhere.

By the same token, Satan is *everywhere* today. Where there is *any kind* of dishonesty, immorality, contention, violence, or addiction, there is Satan. He is in blatant sin; he is in subtle deception. Stay away from him. He is "a roaring lion, [who] walketh about, seeking whom he may devour" (1 Peter 5:8). And he will devour *us*—unless we "put on the whole armour [or power] of God, that [we] may be able to stand against the wiles of the devil" (Ephesians 6:11). For the power of God is stronger than the power of Satan.

Indeed, the power of God and the power of Satan are as different as night and day. Satan's power is temporary and will end (in fact, he's running out of time, and he knows it, which is why his devices are more desperate and extreme than ever before); God's power is absolute and endless. Satan uses his power to destroy and damn; God uses His power to bless, sanctify, and exalt. Satan's arrogance blinds him as well as those who follow him; God is all-seeing and all-knowing. Satan abandons those he spiritually maims, while God has promised to make all of His faithful children "joint-heirs with Christ" (Romans 8:17).

There is only one thing the power of God and the power of Satan have in common: Neither can influence us unless *we* allow them to. The devil can't *make* us do anything. Said the Prophet Joseph: "Satan cannot seduce us by his enticements unless we in our hearts consent and yield" (Ehat and Cook, eds., *Words of Joseph Smith,* 65). On the other hand, although God could manipulate us, He never has and never will. We are free to "choose . . . eternal life, through the great Mediator of all men, or to choose captivity and death, according to the . . . power of the devil" (2 Nephi 2:27). In short, *the kind of power operating in our lives is entirely up to us.*

If God wants a powerful people who can withstand the wiles of the devil (and He does), and if we were born to lead in these latter days (and we were), then we need to understand how God makes His power available to us, and how we gain access to that power.

Here are some of the ways God makes His power available to us:

1. *There is power in the word of God.*

Alma and the sons of Mosiah learned that the preaching of the word—meaning the gospel of Jesus Christ—has a "more powerful effect upon the minds of the people than the sword, or anything else." Alma implored his people to "try the virtue of the word of God" (Alma 31:5). There is power in the word to heal our wounded souls (Jacob 2:8), to help us overcome temptation (1 Nephi 11:25), to prompt us to repent (Jarom 1:12), to humble us (Alma 32:14), to help us overcome the natural man (Mosiah 3:19), to bring about a mighty change in our hearts (Alma 5:13), and to lead us to Christ.

President Boyd K. Packer taught that "true doctrine, understood, changes attitudes and behavior. The study of the doctrines of the gospel will improve behavior quicker than a study of behavior will improve behavior" ("Little Children," 17). In other words, the word of God can lead us to change. It can literally transform us.

I have a lifelong friend whose teenage tampering with pornography evolved into a deadly addiction, and for years it has ruled him and ravaged his marriage. Frankly, I had lost hope that he would ever really change.

And then, a couple of years ago, a remarkable sequence of events began to unfold. He began reading the scriptures for the first time since his mission. The word of God pierced his heart, and he knew he had to repent—which involved heart-wrenching confessions and subsequent excommunication. Now he is working his way back by immersing himself in the gospel as never before. He was recently rebaptized in a sweet and tender service where all present witnessed the power of the Atonement of Jesus Christ to truly change, heal, and cleanse a repentant sinner.

While my friend was working toward rebaptism, he wrote this: "It was when I began to study the gospel that I realized I had been under Satan's power for years. When I finally got on my knees, pleaded for help to change, and surrendered my sins to the Lord, my world turned upside down. This past year has been a crash course in the ways of God and His Son. It has been the most difficult but wonderful year of my life. I wish I could tell everyone who is in a situation like I was to not be afraid to surrender to the Lord. They will find joy like never before in His Atonement. They will feel the Father wrap His arms around them. They will discover there is power in the gospel to really change."

Some may be skeptical about this man's transformation, believing that "once addicted, always addicted." But that is simply not true. The gospel has the power to cleanse and make new, because the word is "quick and powerful," it "divide[s] asunder all the cunning and the snares and the wiles of the devil," and it "lead[s] the man of Christ" in a straight and narrow path away from the gulf of misery prepared by

Satan to engulf the wicked (Helaman 3:29). The Atonement is *real*. My friend is evidence of that. His great change is the change that comes with conversion.

Do *we* know what we believe? Do we know there is power in the doctrine of Christ to change and overcome weakness? Do we realize that the scriptures contain the answer to every life dilemma? A casual understanding of the gospel will not sustain us through the days ahead, which is why it is imperative that we immerse ourselves in the word of God.

In all of scripture, nowhere are the doctrines of the gospel more fully taught than in the Book of Mormon. The Prophet Joseph declared that "a man would get nearer to God by abiding by its precepts, than by any other book" (*History of the Church*, 4:461).

President Ezra Taft Benson repeatedly urged us to immerse ourselves in a serious, ongoing study of this book, making among many others the following promise: "It is not just that the Book of Mormon teaches us truth, though it indeed does that. It is not just that the Book of Mormon bears testimony of Christ, though it indeed does that, too. . . . There is a power in the book which will begin to flow into your lives the moment you begin a serious study of the book" ("Book of Mormon—Keystone of Our Religion," 7).

Parley P. Pratt described this very process. Prior to meeting Hyrum Smith, who first gave him a copy of the Book of Mormon, he had been an avid student of the Bible and a seeker of truth. This is how he described his first encounter with the Book of Mormon: "I read all day; eating was a burden, I had no desire for food; sleep was a burden when the night came, for I preferred reading to sleep. As I read, the spirit of the Lord was upon me, and I knew and comprehended that the book was true. . . . My joy was now full, . . . and I rejoiced sufficiently to more than pay me for all the sorrows, sacrifices, and toils of my life" (*Autobiography of Parley P. Pratt,* 32).

There is power in the word, and nowhere is the word more persuasively or powerfully taught than in the Book of Mormon, which a latter-day prophet has promised will bring power into our lives.

2. There is power in the gift of the Holy Ghost.

The gift of the Holy Ghost is a gift of power. The Holy Ghost inspires and heals, guides and warns, enhances our natural capacities, inspires charity and humility, makes us smarter than we are, strengthens us during trials, testifies of the Father and the Son, and shows us all things that we should do (see 2 Nephi 32:5).

Because the Holy Ghost will show us everything we should do, it only makes sense to learn how He communicates—or to learn the language of revelation. Our challenge is not getting the Lord to speak to us; our challenge is understanding what He has to say (see D&C 6:14).

I remember a time when I was desperate for guidance on a crucial decision. I had fasted and prayed and been to the temple, but the answer wasn't clear. In frustration I told a friend that I just couldn't get an answer. He responded, simply: "Have you asked the Lord to teach you *how* He communicates with you?" I hadn't, so I began to pray daily that He would.

Not long thereafter, while reading about Nephi building the ship that would carry his family across an ocean, I couldn't help but notice how clearly he understood the Lord's instructions. With that, I began to hunt for scriptural evidences of direct communication between God and man. At each one I made a little red *x* in the margin of my scriptures. Now, many years later, my scriptures are littered with little red *x*'s, each an indication that the Lord *does* communicate with His people—and often. The scriptures are the handbook for the language of revelation. They are our personal Liahona. If we will regularly immerse ourselves in the scriptures, we'll get clearer, more frequent answers to our prayers.

Learning this language takes time. As a young captain charged with leading the Nephite armies, Moroni sent messengers to the prophet Alma, asking him to inquire of the Lord where the armies should go. But in time, Moroni received inspiration for his stewardship himself. For he became "a man of a perfect understanding" (Alma 48:11)—suggesting that he learned to speak the language of revelation, perhaps even perfectly.

What a gift, to have access to a pure source of information, a source devoid of flattery or spin-doctoring, for "the Spirit speaketh the truth and lieth not" (Jacob 4:13). The Lord will teach us directly as much truth as we are worthy and willing to learn, for as Elder Bruce R. McConkie taught, "There is *no limit* to the revelations [we] may receive" (*New Witness for the Articles of Faith*, 490; emphasis added).

Having the Holy Ghost as our constant guide and protector is essential to latter-day leadership. The gift of the Holy Ghost is a gift of power.

3. There is power in the priesthood.

By definition, priesthood power is the power and authority of God delegated to men on earth. Those who hold the priesthood have the right to say what the Lord would say if He were here. Whatever they bind on earth is bound in heaven.

Because the priesthood was restored, we have access to ordinances—baptism and confirmation, sealings and healings and blessings, miracles and the ministering of angels. Indeed, the "keys of all the spiritual blessings of the church" (D&C 107:18) are available through the power and authority of the Melchizedek Priesthood.

There is *power* in ordinances. All who are baptized and receive the Holy Ghost are eligible to speak the words of Christ and qualify for eternal life. Those who are endowed with power in the House of the Lord need never face the adversary alone. Couples worthy to be sealed at an altar in that holy house are gifted with power. The power of the priesthood heals, protects, and inoculates every righteous man and woman against the powers of darkness.

I will never forget an experience in Cali, Colombia. After a long evening of meetings, the presiding officer asked the congregation to remain seated while we departed. But upon the final "amen," several dozen priesthood leaders jumped to their feet and formed two lines, creating a pathway from the chapel outside to a waiting van. As we walked through this sheltered passageway, where priesthood leaders symbolized priesthood power, I was deeply moved by the metaphor. For it is the power of the priesthood that marks, clears, and protects the path leading to eternal life. Priesthood power safeguards us from the world, binds heaven and earth, subdues the adversary, blesses and heals, and enables us to triumph over mortality. Every ordinance of the Melchizedek Priesthood helps prepare us to live in the presence of God. As President Harold B. Lee taught, "Through the priesthood and only the priesthood may we . . . find our way back home" (BYU *Speeches of the Year,* 1956, 2).

I am deeply grateful for the power of the priesthood and the gift of having full access to this power, which when used righteously is the only true power on earth.

4. There is power in the House of the Lord.

It is precisely because of priesthood power, the fulness of which is available only in the temple, that we may be endowed with power in the House of the Lord. The Prophet Joseph made this clear at the Kirtland

Temple dedication when he prayed that "thy servants may go forth from this house armed with thy power" (D&C 109:22).

For years now I have attended the temple frequently. It is a place of refuge and revelation. I could never have handled the pressures of recent years without regular time there. This past year, however, a head-banging, hand-wringing challenge has driven me to attend even more. There have been weeks when the only peace I felt was in the temple. Even still, about six months ago, nine words from First Nephi leaped off the page: "And I, Nephi, did go into the mount oft" (1 Nephi 18:3). Instantly I knew I needed to spend even more time in the temple, so I have. The results have not been what I expected. Although I have received help with the challenge in question, it seems that the Lord simply needed me to be in the temple more where it is easier to learn certain things. That was apparently Nephi's experience as well, for as he went unto the mount oft the Lord "showed unto [him] great things"— undoubtedly great things of the Spirit.

In the temple we learn how to deal with Satan, how to live in the world without letting it stain us, how to fulfill our foreordained missions, how to cope with suffocating pressure and heartache, and how to come into the presence of God. The best place to learn about the temple is in the temple. Our kept covenants will eventually save us. And *that* is power!

5. There is power in the Atonement of Jesus Christ.

Until I was in my thirties, I thought the Atonement was basically for sinners—meaning that it allowed us to repent. But then I suffered a heartbreaking personal loss and began to learn that there was so much more to this sublime doctrine. My solution initially to my heartbreak was to exercise so much faith that the Lord would have to give me what I wanted—which was a husband.

Well, the Lord hasn't even yet given me a husband, but He did heal my heart. And in doing so, He taught me that He not only paid the price for sin but compensated for all of the pain we experience in life. Because of His Atonement, we have access to His grace, or enabling power, and to His redemptive power—power that frees us from sin; power to be healed emotionally, physically, and spiritually; power to loose the bands of death (Alma 7:12, 13); power to do good works; power to turn weakness into strength (Ether 12:27); and power to receive salvation through faith on His name (Mosiah 3:19). It is because of the Atonement that if we build our foundation on Christ, the devil can have no power over us (see Helaman 5:12).

It is because of the power and reach of the Atonement that we can triumph over death and rise again, as President Gordon B. Hinckley so poignantly stated in his message at the funeral of Elder Neal A. Maxwell, which he delivered just three months after the death of his own wife. He acknowledged that only those who have experienced the loss of a spouse can understand the "absolute devastation and consuming loneliness, which increases in intensity and gnaws at one's very soul." But then he added that in the still of the night comes a voice that whispers, "all is well, all is well, with a peace, certainty and unwavering affirmation that death is not the end" and that "as surely as there has been separation, there will be a joyful reuniting" (*Deseret Morning News,* 28 July 2004).

There is power in God the Father and His Son Jesus Christ—power that we may access through the Word, the Holy Ghost, the priesthood, and the ordinances of the holy temple.

What then must we do to access this power? First, we must have faith. Faith is the first principle of the gospel because faith is a principle of power that influences, at least to some degree, the Lord's intervention in our lives.

By faith Noah built an ark and saved his posterity, Sarah gave birth "when she was past age" (Hebrews 11:11), Moses parted the Red Sea, Alma and Amulek were delivered from captivity, and the sons of Helaman were miraculously preserved. So great was the faith of the fourteen-year-old Joseph Smith that when he went into a grove of trees and asked "in faith, nothing wavering" (James 1:6), the Father and the Son appeared, ushering in the Restoration.

Faith is a principle of power, which explains why President Hinckley has repeatedly declared that "if there is any one thing you and I need in this world it is faith" ("God Shall Give unto You Knowledge by His Holy Spirit," 109). Our prophet knows whereof he speaks.

Soon after President Hinckley was called to serve as a counselor to President Spencer W. Kimball, the health of the prophet and his two other counselors failed, leaving President Hinckley to shoulder the burdens of the presidency alone. At one point he recorded: "The responsibility I carry frightens me. . . . Sometimes I could weep with concern. But there comes the assurance that the Lord put me here for His purpose, and if I will be humble and seek the direction of the Holy Spirit, He will use me . . . to accomplish His purposes" (Dew, *Go Forward with Faith*, 393). Throughout his life, President Hinckley's practice has been simply to go forward with faith.

Prophets ancient and modern stand as witnesses that the Lord will indeed use His matchless power to help us. Surely the Brother of Jared's transcendent privilege of seeing the Lord was linked to his expression of faith: "I know, O Lord, that thou hast all power, and can do whatsoever thou wilt for the benefit of man; therefore touch these stones. . . .

O Lord, thou canst do this" (Ether 3:4–5). In this instance, as in many others, a person's faith allowed the Lord to do not just what was asked of Him but much more.

Challenges that tax our faith are usually opportunities to stretch and strengthen our faith by finding out if we really believe the Lord will help us.

If your faith is wobbly, if you're not sure the Lord will come to *your* aid, experiment, put Him to the test. "Even if ye can no more than desire to believe, let this desire work in you" (Alma 32:27). A great place to start is in the scriptures, for as Jacob wrote: "We search the prophets, and we have many revelations . . . and having all these witnesses we obtain a hope, and our faith becometh unshaken" (Jacob 4:6).

Unshaken faith activates the power of God in our lives, "for he worketh by power, according to the faith of the children of men" (Moroni 10:7).

Second, we must repent. Faith in Jesus Christ leads us to repent, or turn away from sins that hold us spiritually captive, and to obey with exactness. Great power follows those who repent and obey.

Lamoni's father pledged to "give away" *all* his sins to know God (Alma 22:18). Undoubtedly, every one of us has sins he or she needs to give away. An important question, then, is: What favorite sins, large or small, are you willing to give away—right now, today—in order to increase your access to the power of God? If you want to be sanctified, repentance is not optional.

In contrast to sin, which is ugly and costly, obedience is brilliant and its fruits are endless, one of which is happiness. *The only way to be happy is to live the gospel.*

It is not possible to sin enough to be happy. It is not possible to buy enough to be happy, or to entertain or indulge ourselves enough to be happy. Happiness and joy come only when we are living up to who we are. King Benjamin clearly understood this when he admonished us to "consider on the blessed and happy state of those that keep the commandments of God. For . . . they are blessed in all things, . . . and if they hold out faithful to the end . . . they may dwell with God in a state of neverending happiness" (Mosiah 2:41).

Satan no doubt bristles at this principle, for happiness is something the ultimate narcissist will *never* experience. I have yet to meet people who were happier because they were dishonest, or because they were addicted to something, or because they were immoral. The Lord has blessed us with covenants that keep us on the straight and narrow path because this road less traveled is actually the easier road. It is *so much* easier to be righteous than to sin.

The happiest people I know are those who repent regularly and obey. And a major reason for their happiness is that they have increased access to the power of God.

The third thing we can do to increase the power of God in our lives is to diligently seek. There is perhaps no more frequent invitation or reassuring promise in all of scripture than this one: "Seek me diligently and ye shall find me; ask, and ye shall receive; knock, and it shall be opened unto you" (D&C 88:63).

Notice that God never said, "Seek me a zillion times. Beg again and again. And maybe, just maybe, if you're lucky, I'll help you a little." To the contrary, the two greatest of all Beings are ever ready to help us. No call waiting. No voice mail. In the words of John, "This is the confidence that we have in him, that, if we ask any thing according to his will, he heareth us" (1 John 5:14).

Nonetheless, neither the Father nor His Son will force anything upon us. Though they want to help us by giving us power, how much power we learn to access is entirely up to us.

Most of the revelations received by the Prophet Joseph came after diligent seeking, including this magnificent promise: "I, the Lord, . . . *delight* to honor those who serve me in righteousness. . . . Great shall be their reward and eternal shall be their glory. And to them will I reveal all mysteries. . . . And their wisdom shall be great, and their understanding reach to heaven. . . . For . . . by my power will I make known unto them the secrets of my will" (D&C 76:5–10). Clearly, there is no limit to what the Lord is willing to teach and give us.

The question, then, for you and me is, How much power do we want to have, and what are we willing to do to obtain it? Heber C. Kimball said that "the greatest torment [the Prophet Joseph] had . . . was because this people would not live up to their [spiritual] privileges. . . . He said sometimes that he felt pressed upon and as though he were pent up in an acorn shell, and all because the people did not and would not prepare themselves to receive the rich treasures of wisdom and knowledge that he had to impart. He could have revealed a great many things to us if we had been ready" (in *Journal of Discourses,* 10:167).

Spiritual privileges that call forth the powers of heaven are available to *all* who diligently seek them. The question, then, is, *Will we diligently seek?* Listen to this classic passage from Alma: "*Whosoever will* come may come and partake of the waters of life freely; and whosoever will not come the same is not compelled to come" (Alma 42:27; emphasis added). Notice it doesn't say that just the popular ones or the smart ones on full scholarship or the ones who got married at twenty-one may come. It says *whosoever will*—meaning, it is our choice.

Those who serve missions don't ask investigators, Would you like to come to Church? Would you like to be baptized? They ask, *Will you come? Will you* be baptized?

So may I ask, *Will you* increase your faith? *Will you* repent and obey? *Will you* diligently seek? *Will you* learn to access the power of God so that you can live up to the heavenly recommendation that placed you here now? *Will you do what you were born to do?*

In his last major address as Prime Minister, and while World War II still raged in the Pacific, Winston Churchill said this to his countrymen: "I told you hard things at the beginning of [this war]; you did not shrink, and I should be unworthy of your confidence . . . if I did not still cry; Forward, unflinching, unswerving, indomitable, till the whole task is done and the whole world is safe and clean" (Cannadine, *Speeches of Winston Churchill*, 266).

Perhaps these pages share hard things. But perhaps they also bring a feeling of reassurance that if we will learn to draw upon the power of God, we will not shrink. We will go forward, unflinching, unswerving, indomitable, making the world safer and cleaner, until we've done everything we were born to do. For *we were born to lead*. We were born to build Zion. *We were born for glory.* Everything we do in life should be measured against this grand standard.

In 1894 President Wilford Woodruff said this: "The Almighty is with this people. We shall have all the revelations that we will need, if we will do our duty and obey the commandments of God. . . . The eyes of God and all the holy prophets are watching us. This is the great dispensation that has been spoken of ever since the world began. We are gathered together . . . by the power and commandment of God. . . . Let us fill our mission" (in Clark, comp., *Messages of the First Presidency,* 3:258).

President Gordon B. Hinckley said it this way: "You can be a leader. You *must* be a leader . . . in those causes for which the Church stands. . . . The adversary of all truth would put into your heart a reluctance to make an effort. Cast that fear aside and be valiant in the cause of truth and righteousness" (*Church News,* 21 September 1996, 3).

Yes, these are the days in which a true leader wants to live. In our day, opportunities to change lives and even destinies are nearly endless. We *are* running the anchor leg of the relay. Because *we were born to lead. We were born for glory.*

In the words of Moroni, I commend you to seek this Jesus of whom the apostles and prophets have written (see Ether 12:41) so that you can experience for yourself the *power* in Jesus Christ to strengthen you, to sanctify you, to help you run this leg of the relay. Don't *ever* underestimate the power of Jesus Christ to help you. Isaiah said it this way: "Hast thou not known? hast thou not heard, that the everlasting God, . . . the Creator of the ends of the earth . . . giveth power to the faint; and to them that have no might he increaseth strength. . . . They that wait upon the Lord shall renew their strength; they shall mount up with wings as eagles; they shall run, and not be weary; and they shall walk, and not faint" (Isaiah 40:28–31).

I have learned for myself that this is true. Because of our Father and His Son, we don't have to run this last strenuous leg of the relay alone. We have access to the greatest and grandest of all power. And when we have the power of God with us, we truly can do all things—including everything we were born to do. *And we were born to lead. We were born for glory.*

CHAPTER SEVEN

Bridging the Gaps

Life is a "consecration camp," a time for us to decide who and what we
will become. It is a time for us to determine and demonstrate by our
actions whether or not we want to be part of the kingdom of God—
both here and hereafter—more than we want anything else.

O N A RECENT TRIP TO New York City, three friends and I
caught a subway one evening to Brooklyn and enjoyed a
leisurely walk back into the city across the storied
Brooklyn Bridge, which spans the East River and connects the island of
Manhattan with Brooklyn. As a farm girl raised in the landlocked flat-
lands of the Midwest, I find bridges both unnerving and fascinating. It's
always a little eerie to be suspended high above some crevice or water-
way below, but fascinating that man has found ways to devise such
passageways. I never cease to be amazed at the engineering of those
enormous pillars and towers that are sunk deep enough to hold the
bridge stable regardless of weather, currents, and weight load.

The Brooklyn Bridge was constructed over a period of thirteen years in the face of enormous difficulties. When it was completed in 1883, it had cost some fifteen million dollars and nearly thirty lives—including the life of its original designer, John Roebling, and the health of his son, who took over as chief engineer and suffered a crippling attack of the bends during a diving exploration. At the time of its completion, this bridge was the first steel cable suspension bridge and was 50 percent larger than any other suspension bridge. Its construction demanded the invention of many key materials, including wire rope. Today some 150,000 cars cross the bridge daily, and that number doesn't include the thousands who cross daily on foot and bicycles. Most who cross, even at night when the well-lit bridge seems even more dynamic and imposing, never have cause to think for even a second about what it took to build the bridge they enjoy that spans a river.

Bridges are magnificent devices designed to carry us over various kinds of gaps in the earth's structure—rivers, streams, canyons, gorges, and the like. There are other kinds of gaps, however, that each of us must find ways to bridge.

In the October 2000 general conference, Elder Dallin H. Oaks alluded to this phenomenon: "The Savior confirmed the importance of being converted, even for those with a testimony of the truth. In the sublime instructions given at the Last Supper, He told Simon Peter, 'I have prayed for thee, that thy faith fail not: and when thou art converted, strengthen thy brethren' (Luke 22:32).

"In order to strengthen his brethren . . . this man who had followed Jesus for three years, who had been given the authority of the holy apostleship, who had been a valiant teacher and testifier of the Christian gospel, and whose testimony had caused the Master to declare him blessed still had to be 'converted.'

"Jesus' challenge shows that the conversion He required for those who would enter the kingdom of heaven . . . was far more than just being converted to the truthfulness of the gospel. . . . The gospel challenges us . . . to *do* and to *become*" (in *Conference Report,* October 2000, 42; emphasis in original).

As Elder Oaks taught us about the process of becoming true followers of Jesus Christ, of laying down our nets and following Him, he invited us to practice what we believe rather than to just preach what we believe. In other words, he invited us to identify the gaps in our lives and to consider how to bridge them. When the Savior spoke to Simon Peter, he identified a natural gap we all deal with: the gap between what we say we believe and the way we actually live.

The mortal experience is filled with gaps:

- between what we know and what we do
- between the ways of God and the ways of man
- between preaching and practicing
- between what the media represents and what really occurred
- between what the media popularizes and what the Lord endorses
- between what we know to be true and how willing we are to stand up for what we believe
- between the world's standard of morality and God's law of chastity
- between the world's definition of the family and God's divine plan for the family

And on it goes. For each of us, there are gaps with which to deal. For example, if you believe the Word of Wisdom but don't fully live it, there's a gap. If you believe your family is the most important entity on earth but often seem to get pulled elsewhere, there's a gap. There are gaps if you feel love for your spouse but withhold love for some reason, if you want a strong marriage but don't make building it a priority, if you believe modesty is important but are tired of coaching teenagers who are tempted to wear clothes that are too tight, too short, too revealing, and with slits up to high heaven, and therefore you say nothing. There are gaps if you say money isn't everything but spend your time and energy as though it were; if you believe in a living prophet but manage to slip away most conference weekends to the beach or the lake; if you believe there is power in the word of God but don't spend much time immersed in the scriptures . . . and so on.

Now, before we go on, let me clarify that *I am not* calling for some kind of unrealistic expectation of perfection that only leaves us feeling that we're falling short. Gaps are a fundamental mortal condition, and thus the process of closing those gaps is a fundamental mortal exercise.

In fact, there is reason to think of conversion—which is rarely something that happens as a blinding, stunning, single event, or as a moment we can mark in time—as the process of narrowing and eventually closing gaps. True conversion takes a lifetime, and perhaps longer.

When my sister entered the Missionary Training Center in Provo, Utah, at the famous introductory meeting (where at the end the missionaries exit through one door and the families through another), the MTC president said: "Our missionaries sometimes joke about the MTC being a concentration camp. But we like to think of it as a *consecration* camp."

Actually, *life* is a consecration camp, a time for us to decide who and what we will become. It is a time for us to determine and demonstrate by our actions whether or not we want to be part of the kingdom of

God—both here and hereafter—more than we want anything else. It is a time to become truly and completely converted.

And the process of conversion, as stated earlier, is one of closing the gaps.

This process *should not discourage us*. It should not alarm us. It should not dishearten us. It is integral to the mortal experience.

Remember Nephi? He had already believed his father's words and sought his own vision, which he had received; seen angels; built a ship, without any prior experience, not after the manner of man; been tied to the mast of a ship and finally cut down; chopped off Laban's head at the express instruction of the Lord; and demonstrated phenomenal faith even when his parents' faith had momentarily wavered. And yet, he offered this lament: "O wretched man that I am! Yea, my heart sorroweth because of my flesh; my soul grieveth because of mine iniquities. I am encompassed about, because of the temptations and the sins which do so easily beset me. And when I desire to rejoice, my heart groaneth because of my sins" (2 Nephi 4:17–19).

Even Nephi, who was both faithful and filled with faith, wrestled with the struggle of mortality and anguished over his performance from time to time. Further, the more he pondered the things of God, the more sensitive he became to his own weaknesses and shortcomings.

But as he wrestled, he learned and grew and experienced again, from time to time, the mercies of the Lord. Consider these words of reflection: "Why should I yield to sin, because of my flesh? Yea, why should I give way to temptations. . . . Awake, my soul! No longer droop in sin. Rejoice" (2 Nephi 4:27–28).

Here's a little secret: As the gap narrows, the very fact that you are dealing with a gap troubles you even more. At the same time, however, the joy of having the Lord insert Himself in between you and the adversary becomes more obvious, more apparent, more joyous.

Consider Joseph Smith. Three and a half years after his transcendent experience in that grove of trees in upstate New York, when he saw both the Father and the Son, he lamented: "I frequently fell into many foolish errors, and displayed the weakness of youth, and the foibles of human nature; which, I am sorry to say, led me into divers temptations, offensive in the sight of God" (Joseph Smith–History 1:28). That was the first prophet of this dispensation! We all know his story, and how he constantly grew in the gospel. Yet in a letter to Emma he wrote: "I call to mind all the past moments of my life and am left to mourn and shed tears of sorrow for my folly" (as quoted in Madsen, *The Highest in Us*, 85).

President Spencer W. Kimball was forthright about the agony he experienced upon being called to the holy apostleship. He recorded in his journal: "My weakness overcame me again. Hot tears came flooding down my cheeks as I made no effort to mop them up. I was accusing myself, and condemning myself and upbraiding myself. I was praying aloud for special blessings from the Lord. I was telling Him that I had not asked for this position, that I was incapable of doing the work, that I was imperfect and weak and human, that I was unworthy of so noble a calling, though I had tried hard and my heart had been right" (Edward L. Kimball, *Spencer W. Kimball*, 193).

We *all* have gaps in our lives, and particularly the gap between what we know and how we live. This gap should not discourage or alarm us, but it should concern us. In fact, it should arguably be the greatest concern of our lives.

We aren't likely to find perfection in this life. At least, the Prophet

Joseph said we wouldn't. "When you climb up a ladder," he taught, "you must begin at the bottom, and ascend step by step, until you arrive at the top; and so it is with the principles of the Gospel—you must begin with the first, and go on until you learn all the principles of exaltation. But it will be a great while after you have passed through the veil before you will have learned them. . . . It will be a great work to learn our salvation and exaltation even beyond the grave" (*Teachings of the Prophet Joseph Smith*, 348).

Thus, achieving perfection in mortality is not the goal. But narrowing the gap, however large it is, between what we know and how we live, is the goal. The million-dollar question is: How do we do that?

There are many principles and pursuits that can help us, but in this chapter, let us focus on just one. We have been given a gift that, when accepted and utilized, can help us more than any other. That gift is the gift and the power of the Holy Ghost. If we learn what the Holy Ghost is able and prepared to do for us, we can gain great strength to live as we believe.

Let's set the stage by clarifying some doctrine as taught by our leaders. President Lorenzo Snow said that it is the "grand privilege of every Latter-day Saint . . . to have the manifestations of the spirit every day of our lives . . . [so] that we may know the light, and not be groveling continually in the dark" (in *Conference Report*, April 1899, 52).

His sister, Eliza R. Snow, the second general president of the Relief Society, said this about the Holy Ghost: "When you are filled with the Spirit of God, and the Holy Ghost rests upon you . . . do you have any trials? I do not think you do. For that satisfies and fills up every longing of the human heart, and fills up every vacuum. When I am filled with that spirit my soul is satisfied; and I can say in good earnest, that the trifling things of the day do not seem to stand in my way at all. But just let me lose my hold on that spirit and power of the Gospel, and partake of the spirit of the world, in the slightest degree, and trouble comes; there is something wrong. . . . And is it not our privilege to so live that we can have this constantly flowing into our souls?" (*Woman's Exponent*, vol. 2, no. 8 [15 September 1873]: 62).

Every week, as we partake of the emblems of the sacrament, we are promised that if we will do three things—take the name of the Lord upon us, always remember Him, and keep His commandments—we may *always* have His Spirit to be with us (see Moroni 4:3). This becomes crucial to us when we consider what President John Taylor taught: "I do not care how learned a man may be, or how extensively he may have traveled. I do not care what his talent, intellect, or genius may be, at what college he may have studied, how comprehensive his views or what his judgment may be on other matters, he cannot understand certain things without the Spirit of God" (*Gospel Kingdom*, 35).

Very simply, the Holy Ghost can make us smarter, wiser, and more resilient than we inherently are. That is because, among other things, the Holy Ghost will show unto us all things that we should do. Imagine how ironclad, how encompassing that promise is! There are no disclaimers, no limiters, just a phenomenal promise, given to all those who will "enter in by the way, and receive the Holy Ghost" (2 Nephi 32:5).

After he was martyred, the Prophet Joseph appeared to Brigham Young in a dream and gave him instructions: "Tell the brethren to be humble and faithful and be sure to keep the Spirit of the Lord, that it will lead them aright. Be careful and not turn away the still, small voice; it will teach them what to do and where to go. . . . Tell the brethren to keep their hearts open to conviction, so that when the Holy Ghost comes to them, their hearts will be ready to receive it. They can tell the Spirit of the Lord from all other spirits—it will whisper peace and joy to their souls; it will take malice, hatred, strife and all evil from their hearts, and their whole desire will be to do good, bring forth righteousness, and build up the kingdom of God" (*Manuscript History of Brigham Young,* February 23, 1847, as quoted by Marion G. Romney in *Conference Report,* April 1944, 140–41).

In brief, here are just some of the unique things the Holy Ghost is willing and qualified to do for us.

The Holy Ghost is a testifier, with His most important testimony being of the Father and the Son. Our testimonies begin here, with a witness of the Spirit that God is our Father, that Jesus Christ our Savior is His Son, and that He, the Son, stands at the head of the Church. Without the presence and ministering of the Holy Ghost, it would be impossible to gain a personal testimony that the gospel of Jesus Christ has been restored to the earth.

And the Holy Ghost is not only a testifier and a revelator but the Supreme Conversion Agent. He not only testifies of the Father and the Son, and enables us to gain testimonies of them, but will convert us to the gospel, the power of the word of God, the purpose and power of the temple, the purpose and power of fasting and prayer, and on and on.

When the Holy Ghost is involved in the process, the experience of fasting moves from one of going without food to a time of learning how to draw upon the powers of heaven. When the Holy Ghost testifies about what is taking place in the temple, we begin slowly to experience and understand what is taking place there. Until then, it's often basically an exercise in obedience, but as we begin to discover what is there, we can't be kept away. We learn how to pray with greater power. We learn how to deal with the adversary. We learn how to part the veil. And the Translator who helps us understand all these things and more is the Holy Ghost.

The Holy Ghost will show us our weaknesses, enable us to acknowledge them, and then help us overcome them. My experience is that whenever I ask the Lord to reveal my weaknesses to me, He's quick to respond. And there never seems to be a shortage of weaknesses to reveal. But we are all engaged in the exhausting, never-ending process of overcoming the natural man (and woman), and the Holy Ghost is key to that process.

The Holy Ghost prompts us to repent, for the "Lord God called upon men by the Holy Ghost everywhere and commanded them that they should repent" (Moses 5:14). The Holy Ghost *is* the Being who awakens our conscience on matters big and small and presses upon us to repent.

The Holy Ghost is the ultimate teacher, for as the Savior taught His disciples, "the Comforter, which is the Holy Ghost, . . . shall teach you all things, and bring all things to your remembrance" (John 14:26). For "it is given unto many to know the mysteries of God" (Alma 12:9)—meaning the way God works, the peaceable things of the kingdom that can't be learned in a book but are more likely learned when in fasting and prayer, or in the temple, or in times and places of sincere ponder-ing, where the Holy Ghost is present.

Any wise gospel teacher, in any setting, knows that he or she is merely a discussion leader, for the Holy Ghost is He who teaches and instructs in any setting where pure truth is taught. That is His privilege; that is His responsibility. That is why it is crucial that those who endeavor to teach the gospel—in the home, at Church, or in any setting—understand their role, and that seeking to have the Spirit guide and be with them is Job One.

Regardless of how spectacular a presentation might be, if it is delivered without the presence and guidance of the Holy Ghost, it is only a presentation—nothing more. Such a presentation rarely has the ability to sink deep into the hearts of men and women.

On the other hand, even the most simple, modest message delivered under the presence of the Spirit can be profound and illuminating, because "when a man speaketh by the power of the Holy Ghost the power of the Holy Ghost carrieth it unto the hearts of the children of men" (2 Nephi 33:1).

I've experienced for myself how deadly it is to stand in front of an audience when I haven't made the suitable preparations to make sure that my message was both developed and presented under the direction of the Spirit. Such a presentation is a dreadful experience for all present.

On the other hand, when the Spirit is present it is an unequaled adventure, privilege, and teaching and learning experince. For, as many people have stated, when you teach by the Spirit, you inevitably say things or make connections or draw parallels you've never even considered before.

The Holy Ghost inspires charity and selfless love. The pure love of Christ is conveyed by the Holy Ghost. Further, the Spirit of the Lord cannot dwell where there is contention, judging, blaming, or unhealthy, ego-motivated competition. The Spirit is what fills us with charity as opposed to the craving to compete, dominate, and subdue. The Spirit also inspires tenderness and humility, which are both natural extensions of the pure love of Christ.

The Holy Ghost enables us to forgive—to forgive ourselves, and to forgive others. It is impossible to truly forgive someone who has hurt or wounded us without the presence of the Holy Ghost in our lives.

The Holy Ghost is the force that binds relationships—marriages, friendships, family ties. Beyond that, He heals relationships, tempers emotions, and helps us see things as they really are.

The Holy Ghost is the Comforter, and brings comfort and peace to our souls in even the most distressing of times—or perhaps we should say, *particularly* in the most distressing of times. He will strengthen us during trials, help us overcome difficulties, and enable us to deal with more than we would ever be able to deal with on our own. In this regard, He enhances any natural abilities and gifts we have. He makes us smarter, more creative, more talented, more patient, more intelligent, and more persistent. The operative word here, of course, is *more*. He helps us do more and become more than we could ever manage on our own.

The Holy Ghost prompts, warns, and guides, for the Lord will "tell you in your mind and in your heart, by the Holy Ghost, which shall come upon you and which shall dwell in your heart. Now, behold, this is the spirit of revelation" (D&C 8:2–3). Those promptings to turn around, go a different direction, change course—be they literal or figurative—all come from the Holy Ghost as we seek after such guidance, protection, and direction.

The Holy Ghost increases our discernment and enables us to distinguish truth from error and distortion. How crucial this is today, when essentially every form of media is filled to some degree with subtle deceptions.

Satan is the master of illusion and distraction. He is the master of making evil appear good, and good appear evil and unsophisticated. He makes dangerous things appear exciting rather than forbidden. He makes things seem important that are not, and completely undermines the significance of the few things that really do matter.

The Holy Ghost is the ultimate antidote to Satan on every front. He helps us see through even Satan's most subtle deceptions and illusions and exposes them for what they are.

The Holy Ghost makes it possible for us to receive personal revelation, as the Lord explained to Hyrum Smith in a revelation through his brother, the Prophet Joseph: "I will impart unto you of my Spirit, which shall enlighten your mind, which shall fill your soul with joy," Hyrum was told. "And then shall ye know, or by this shall you know, all things whatsoever you desire of me, which are pertaining unto things of righteousness" (D&C 11:13–14).

The Holy Ghost is the ultimate Translator, the ultimate Revelator, the ultimate purveyor of knowledge, as Ammon taught King Lamoni when he said: "A portion of that Spirit dwelleth in me, which giveth me knowledge, and also power according to my faith and desires which are in God" (Alma 18:35). It is precisely because of His willingness to work in our lives that it is possible for us to receive instructions, via personal revelation, from our Father.

The Holy Ghost can actually affect our physical appearance. I've heard it said that at the age of twenty we have the face we were born with, but at the age of seventy we have the face we deserve—a face that reflects the kind of life we have lived.

I have often had the experience of being with men and women whose lives reflect decades of goodness and obedience. Sometimes I catch myself staring at such people, for truly, regardless of their physical attributes, they are beautiful and filled with light. Parley P. Pratt said that the Holy Ghost "develops beauty of person, form, and features" (*Key to the Science of Theology,* 61). I believe it. I don't think there is any woman more beautiful than one who is filled with the Holy Ghost, or a man more appealing than one who is immersed in the Spirit.

The Holy Ghost gradually helps reveal to us who we are, meaning not only who we are today but who we have always been. Thus, He helps us deal with our mortal identity crises.

The world, under Satan's control, does everything imaginable to get us to rate or judge ourselves based upon the criteria of Babylon: wealth, status, privilege, beauty, accomplishment, and so forth. But the Lord sees us differently, and it is the Holy Ghost who reveals that information to us.

Remember when Samuel came to Jesse, having been prompted that among his sons was the future king of Israel? Jesse paraded his sons in front of Samuel, who met them all but felt no inspiration regarding any of them. Finally, he asked Jesse if he had any other sons who weren't there. "Well, there is David," Jesse in essence responded, "who is out in the fields with the sheep." Samuel asked that David be brought before him, at which point the Holy Ghost moved upon Samuel to reveal the divine destiny and mission of David. In one statement, Samuel explained how the Lord views us: "For the Lord seeth not as man seeth; for man looketh on the outward appearance, but the Lord looketh on the heart" (1 Samuel 16:7).

Something similar happened with Enoch, who was shocked when the Lord called him to preach repentance to the people. His initial response was halting and confused: "Why is it that I have found favor in thy sight, and am but a lad, and all the people hate me; for I am slow of speech; wherefore am I thy servant?" (Moses 6:31).

The Lord responded simply by promising Enoch that if he would "go forth and do," and if he would be willing to open his mouth, the Lord would give him utterance and would justify all of his words. "Thou shalt abide in me, and I in you; therefore walk with me" (Moses 6:32, 34).

Enoch may not have had so much as a particle of self-confidence, but he did have faith. And the results were electrifying. For "so great was the faith of Enoch that he led the people of God, and . . . he spake the word of the Lord, and the earth trembled, and the mountains fled, even according to his command; and the rivers of water were turned out of their course; . . . so powerful was the word of Enoch, and so great was the power of the language which God had given him" (Moses 7:13).

Surely Enoch's initial experience with the Lord taught him volumes about who he truly was, as a called son of God, and enabled him in time to overcome entirely any mortal inhibitions and insecurities that may have previously distorted his view of himself.

Joseph Smith came to a time when he also wanted to know how the Lord saw him. After lamenting the errors of his youthful ways, he determined to approach the Lord, that "I might know of my state and standing before him; for I had full confidence in obtaining a divine manifestation, as I previously had" (Joseph Smith–History 1:29). What resulted was a series of four consecutive visits by the Angel Moroni.

Years later, in a glorious declaration, Joseph Smith arose in the Nauvoo Grove in April 1844 and declared that "God himself was once as we are now, and is an exalted man" (*History of the Church*, 6:305).

Clearly the Prophet Joseph's understanding of our divine identity had matured and come full circle.

Lorenzo Snow later taught that "Jesus was a god before he came into this world and yet his knowledge was taken from him. He did not know his former greatness, neither do we know what greatness we had attained to before we came here, but he had to pass through an ordeal, as we have to, without knowing or realizing at the time the greatness and importance of his mission and works" (*Office Journal of Lorenzo Snow,* 8 October 1900, 181–82).

Without question, the Lord seems to delight in calling the weak and simple, by the world's standards, to do His work. He said as much in a revelation to the Prophet Joseph: "Be not weary in well-doing," He commanded, "for ye are laying the foundation of a great work. And out of small things proceedeth that which is great." The Lord then went on to outline His requirements for service in the kingdom, requirements that differ markedly from the world's requirements for greatness: "Behold, the Lord requireth the heart and a willing mind" (D&C 64:33–34).

Alma taught his son Helaman the same thing when he asserted that "by small and simple things are great things brought to pass; and small means in many instances doth confound the wise" (Alma 37:6).

There are countless examples of the Lord's *modus operandi:* Sarah, though advanced in age, bore Isaac, with whom the Lord established the everlasting covenant; barren Elisabeth bore John the Baptist, the Forerunner. A fourteen-year-old boy ushered in the last dispensation. Eliza R. Snow, who never bore a child, served twenty-one years as general president of the Relief Society and also helped organize the Young Women and Primary organizations.

Indeed, overcoming our mortal identity crises and coming to truly

know and believe who we are is essential to closing some of the afore-
mentioned gaps. As we come to sense who we are, our entire lives
change. Our sense of purpose and mission becomes dramatically
focused. Our priorities change. Our attitudes typically begin to moder-
ate about everything from the way we spend our time and money to the
way we *feel* about our time and money. The way we view challenges and
trials typically changes. What is important to us becomes more clear in
our minds. And that is because we begin to "seek the riches which it is
the will of the Father to give unto [us]" (D&C 38:39), the riches of
eternity.

To summarize, the Holy Ghost helps us find and feel true happiness. I have come to believe a fairly simple maxim: Whatever we really
want, we'll probably get. If money is more important to us than anything else, we'll probably find a way to get it. If power is our priority,
the same thing goes. And so on. Certainly Lucifer is hard at work trying
to convince us that the good life is derived from vacations and water
toys and Rolexes and large homes. Not that there is anything wrong
with vacations and water toys and Rolexes and large homes. *However,*
and this is a large however, the ability to see things as they really are
and as they really will be is essential if we are to keep worldly matters
and issues in the proper perspective.

Lucifer clearly had his way with Laman and Lemuel, for they
bought his line that comfort and possessions are connected to joy. They
gave themselves away in one of their many lectures to Nephi: "Thou art
like unto our father, led away by the foolish imaginations of his heart;
yea, . . . we have wandered in the wilderness for these many years; and
our women have toiled, being big with child; and they have borne children in the wilderness and suffered all things. . . . Behold, these many

years we have suffered in the wilderness, which time we might have enjoyed our possessions and the land of our inheritance; yea, and we might have been happy" (1 Nephi 17:20–21). Lucifer had persuaded Laman and Lemuel that comfort and possessions and ease of life resulted in joy.

And yet, the truth is that rarely does anything of the world—a new possession, a new toy, a new anything—result in joy. And that is because joy is carried into the hearts of men and women by the Holy Ghost, who seems to be largely unimpressed by and uninterested in products that roll off the assembly line.

I have visited men and women living in the most humble conditions who were filled with light and who found great joy and happiness in their everyday lives. I'll never forget a series of experiences I had in Africa, where in village after village I met with women who radiated pure happiness. I had similar experiences in the Philippines, and Cambodia, and Ecuador, and the outreaches of Brazil. It is quite possible to be happy without owning much of this world's goods. It is not possible, however, to be truly happy without the abiding, sustaining presence of the Holy Ghost.

This has been a brief (and incomplete) summary of some of the things the Holy Ghost does for us. Every one of these endowments from the Spirit will help us gradually narrow the gap between what we believe and how we live; between who we are and have always been and who we are in the process of becoming.

President George Q. Cannon made it very clear that we all have very specific missions to perform here: "God has chosen us out of the world and has given us a great mission. I do not entertain a doubt myself but that we were selected and fore-ordained for the mission before the world was; that we had our parts allotted to us in this mortal state of existence as our Savior had His assigned to Him" ("Topics of the Times," 140).

Narrowing the gaps in our lives is essential if we are to fulfill our foreordained missions here on earth. And having the Holy Ghost operative in our lives on an ongoing basis is key to narrowing the gaps. It is key to the process of becoming truly converted.

CHAPTER EIGHT

Sin Makes You Stupid, and It Costs a Lot Too

*Our Father wants His children back, and He will go to
great lengths to help them—as evidenced, first and foremost,
by the fact that He gave His Only Begotten Son,
who in turn gave His life.*

THERE IS A MAN I HAVE KNOWN most of his life. I'll call him Jack. He has a great heart, is bright, has a zany sense of humor, and has always had that distinctive quality that makes him the life of the party. As a schoolboy he was great in sports, and he always seemed to be able to keep everyone laughing.

Jack's life changed abruptly, though, when during his teenage years his mother died suddenly. Her death seemed to almost halt Jack's emotional development. As a result, in his later teenage years Jack fell into some unhealthy and in some cases rebellious patterns. In time, his fun sense of humor seemed to disappear, and he became more difficult for family and friends to reach. His ability to reason, to see things as they really were, became impaired, and it often seemed as though he was seeing the world (emotionally and spiritually, at least) through Coke-bottle-thick glasses. As a result, he made a fair number of decisions that weren't very productive ones and had a hard time staying in the center of the straight and narrow path.

Those who know and love Jack had him constantly in their thoughts and prayers, but some—including even members of his own family—admit that they had reached the point where they had stopped praying that he would still consider serving a mission. As the years ticked by, it looked as though that was beyond hope. Most started to pray that he would somehow find his way out of the fog he was in. But the possibility of a mission seemed to disappear entirely.

Then an unexpected sequence of events began to unfold. Some friends affected Jack in uplifting and positive ways. A few family members seemed able to reach him. Jack started working with his bishop, and slowly, little by little, began to reverse the effects of the previous years. Happily, none of his activities or behaviors were such that they had disqualified him from missionary service. And finally, a couple of years later than normal, he entered the mission field.

That two-year period proved a remarkable reversal to the previous years, as his spiritual growth was greater than anyone had imagined or hoped for. Not long before he returned home, he wrote the following: "I can't explain to you how much I have learned. The Book of Mormon has become more real to me. *I'm becoming who I always wanted to be, but didn't know how before. The molding effect that the gospel has on people sure is a true power, if you let it be.*"

When asked what specifically he was learning on his mission that he didn't think he could have learned elsewhere, he replied: "There are so many things I couldn't have learned anywhere else, one of them being the ability to focus more on the things I can control and trust that the Lord will fill in the gaps. The people here have taught me how to be patient and forgiving. I have learned the importance of destroying the pride and sarcasm that I have so much of."

There is no way to relate sufficiently how dramatically this young man changed. When the gospel started to take hold of his life, a literal transformation began. And the miracle only accelerated on his mission.

Prior to his mission, sin (or at least, careless mistakes) had made him stupid, and it had cost a lot too. It had cost him time, self-respect, and relationships he cared about. It cost him opportunities to make progress and move toward goals. It cost him an inner sense of peace about his life. And it cost him confidence—because he had been living beneath himself, and when we live beneath ourselves, it's not possible to feel peace of mind and self-confidence.

Consider again the telling line from his letter: "The molding effect that the gospel has on people sure is a true power, if you let it be." Being immersed in the gospel for nearly two years did things for this young man that nothing else could ever have done.

There are things we can learn from Jack and from others who have let go of the iron rod and taken detours from spiritual safety before once again finding the straight and narrow path. For sin truly does make us stupid. It makes us deaf, dumb, and blind to the ways of the Lord. It makes us stupid in many ways. Those who are unrepentant are typically stupid emotionally and even financially because they can't see what is really happening in their interactions with others. One stupid decision or judgment often leads to another. And sin absolutely wrecks our judgment about what is, or is not, important.

Sin makes us stupid because it drives the Spirit away, which means we're on our own and outside the protective, guiding, inspiring influence of the Holy Ghost. Disobedience, and particularly intentional sin, interrupts and sometimes halts guidance from the Spirit. The Liahona stopped working when Laman and Lemuel bound Nephi.

Sin cultivates pride, which also distorts and deceives. Why did Laman and Lemuel endure four days of incredibly rough seas once they bound Nephi? Because they were too proud to admit their wrongdoing and repent.

In short, repeated sin dulls receptivity to the Spirit. It dulls all righteous emotions and senses. It is simply not possible to indulge in a pattern of willful sin and (1) feel love from others, including the Lord, or (2) give love to others or the Lord. I remember watching one friend make years of bad decisions and choices based upon "how he felt." But he felt the way he did because the cycle of his sinning never stopped. While immersed in sin, he couldn't feel any love for his wife or love from her. He couldn't feel love for other family members, including his children. Nor could he feel the deep love of many who were reaching out to him in an effort to help.

This is the reason that those engaged in an affair can think they are in love, when it really isn't possible to feel real love—the pure love of Christ—while engaged in immoral acts. The lack of the Spirit makes them stupid, allowing Lucifer to present his counterfeit, which is lust and attraction and immediate self-gratification.

Perhaps one of the most spiritually significant facts we could teach our youth is that when we choose to sin, we choose to live on our own, without the power of the Holy Ghost to help us.

Sin costs a lot too. We've all seen the advertisements and promos during the holidays about the gifts that keep on giving. Well, sin is one thing that truly keeps on giving—heartache, hurt, anguish, remorse, pain, shame, and on and on.

Satan is incredibly skilled when it comes to promoting the superficial benefits of sin while temporarily masking its costs. And yet, the only "benefit" of sin, if it can be called a benefit, is momentary gratification. On the other hand, the negative effects of unrepented sin only escalate with time and repetition.

Sin can cost all kinds of things: money, position, jobs, status, family, time, respect, self-respect, integrity, virtue, health, future opportunities, Church membership, relationships, trust of those you love, trust of the Lord, and eternal progression. Most of all, unrepented sin threatens exaltation.

The costs of sin spread far beyond the sinner's life. The person who declares, "It's *my* life. I can live it as I wish," is one who has clearly subscribed to the distortions of Lucifer. It's just not possible for someone to willfully commit sin without having it affect the well-being, the happiness, the lives of others. Perhaps the saddest destruction sin causes is that experienced by the innocent.

It's impossible to quantify the grief wrought by the actions of terrorists. It's impossible to measure the grief of a husband or wife who learns a spouse has been unfaithful, or the pain of a parent who learns that an unmarried teenage daughter is carrying a child, or the sadness, heartache, and sense of hopelessness of a child whose parents separate or divorce because of sin. Truly, the costs of sin are never confined to just one person.

The cost of sin must also be calculated to include all of the positive things that could have been happening in the meantime, but weren't. In the business world, this is referred to as "opportunity cost"—the cost of missed opportunities, the cost of regret.

Without question, sin makes us stupid, and it costs a lot too. Why, then, would we ever fall into sin's trap? One reason is because we don't always recognize sin. Big sins don't start out big—they generally begin as little sins and then escalate.

There are almost always small breaches of integrity and acts of disobedience that precede such things as adultery, fornication, addiction, and abuse. King Benjamin seemed to have the cumulative effects of such a sequence in mind when he counseled his people: "If ye do not watch yourselves, and your thoughts, and your words, and your deeds, and observe the commandments of God, . . . ye must perish" (Mosiah 4:30). Indeed, thoughts typically lead to words, which almost always precede actions or deeds.

Respected psychologist Dr. Carlfred Broderick spoke often about adultery as the sin that came "out of the blue like a scheduled airline." His point, of course, was that adultery is never accidental or unplanned. It's the natural result of certain behaviors and takes almost no effort to predict, given such preparatory behaviors.

On the farm, when my father was ready to break a colt, he'd often have us go through a little sequence to get the colt ready. First, we were supposed to just sit on the fence so that the animal got used to us. Then we were to walk around in the corral and feed the colt. Then we would progress to petting the horse. Once we had reached that point, we could usually put our arm around the animal and slip a halter around its nose and face. Shortly after that a bridle, with a bit placed in the horse's mouth, would follow. At that point, we could lead the horse wherever we wanted him to go. This happened little by little, step by step. There were no big, sudden movements, just small, calculated ones that led to total control of the animal.

Satan works the same way. "The safest road to Hell is the gradual one," wrote C. S. Lewis, "the gentle slope, soft underfoot, without sudden turnings, without milestones, without signposts" (*Screwtape Letters*, 54).

What we see happening in the world at large and in the lives of many who succumb to the deceptions and distortions of the adversary is spelled out clearly in the Book of Mormon, which among many other things is a brilliant handbook on defeating Satan's strategies in the latter days. Nephi clearly explained that the devil would grasp his victims "with his everlasting chains," that in our day he would "rage in the hearts of the children of men, and stir [us] up to anger against that which is good," that he would try to "cheat" our souls and lead us away "carefully down to hell" (just as we did with the young colt), and that he would attempt to convince us there was no hell until he could grasp us with "his awful chains, from whence there is no deliverance" (2 Nephi 28:19–22).

Enoch's vision in which he saw the effects of Satan is chilling: "And he beheld Satan; and he had a great chain in his hand, and it veiled the whole face of the earth with darkness; and he looked up and laughed, and his angels rejoiced" (Moses 7:26).

Someone caught in a cycle of repeated, unrepented sin will find it increasingly difficult to detect the advances and strategies of Satan, because one caught in the middle of such sin is less likely to be able to distinguish good from evil.

Unrepented sin makes us vulnerable to more sin. In the case of a longtime friend of mine, one of the side effects of his addiction to pornography was that it created a constant thirst for self-gratification. This, in turn, led to wild spending, escalating risk-taking, dishonesty, so-called affairs of the heart, and eventually adultery.

Such escalation happens, simply, because once people have breached their integrity, they don't have anything left to fall back on. They can't trust themselves, and they don't even try. The result is often many forms of dishonesty, including lying about the sin itself.

When you hide a sin, or lie about a sin, it seems to almost guarantee that at some point—an hour later, a day later, a week later, ten years later—you will repeat the sin. This pattern becomes a vicious cycle that allows the adversary to increase his hold on his victims and wrap them with those cords and chains that bind.

The only thing that breaks the cycle is confession and repentance. One man I know, who was excommunicated twice over a fifteen-year period of time, went to a series of therapists and priesthood leaders. But nothing changed. When he finally, truly confessed and subsequently repented of all sins, he could begin the process of true conversion. Until then, all of the hacking at the leaves that various counselors and friends had done, in an attempt to help, had no lasting results. The roots of sin were still in place until he completely confessed and repented.

All sin *must* be confessed. That is all there is to it. As Alma taught his son Corianton, "Ye cannot hide your crimes from God; and except ye repent they will stand as a testimony against you at the last day" (Alma 39:8). Sin must be confessed so that the process of repentance can begin and progress can continue.

In a worldwide priesthood leadership address, President Gordon B. Hinckley told the story of a woman who refused a calling from her bishop, much to the bishop's surprise, for this woman had been a faithful member of the Church for decades. Confused at her reluctance to accept the calling, the bishop went to visit her. During their visit he learned that she and her husband had indulged premaritally in sexual sin, and had never confessed doing so. She had felt unclean all those years and still felt unworthy to hold a calling.

Truly, for progression to continue, sin must be confessed—either in private to the Lord, or formally to priesthood leaders, when the circumstances warrant doing so.

Knowing this, it is difficult for us to stand by and watch loved ones caught in the downward spiral of sin. But we cannot compel each other to be humble and repent and change.

We can, however, encourage each other. We can try to be understanding and supportive. We can share insights and bear testimony. We can implore. And most important, we can plead with the Lord in someone else's behalf; we can fast and pray that their hearts will be softened and that circumstances will arise to humble and teach them. But all of the nagging and lecturing in the world cannot force someone else to take the steps necessary to repent and change.

I am convinced, however, that when we fast and pray for someone who is trapped in a cycle of disobedience, the Lord is more able to work miracles in that person's life. Alma's reaction to the news that his son had been stricken dumb is revealing: "And they rehearsed unto his father all that had happened unto them; *and his father rejoiced,* for he knew that it was the power of God" (Mosiah 27:20; emphasis added).

Surely Alma had prayed and pleaded with the Lord for many days, over many years, to intervene in the life of his troubled son. His efforts were at least partly (and perhaps largely) responsible for the miracle of conversion that subsequently occurred.

Responding to our pleas, the Lord often brings about circumstances, in His own way and time, designed to reach His children. I think of a husband and wife who had struggled in their marriage for decades. There had been contention, mistrust, and eventually infidelity. Loved ones and friends had tried in countless ways to help them, but circumstances only seemed to get worse. Finally, after much fasting and prayer, the wife felt that divorce was the only answer. What she didn't know was that, at the same time, other things were transpiring to soften her husband's heart.

Her request for a divorce coincided almost perfectly with her husband's silent pleadings to the Lord for help to some way work his way back from decades of serious sin and misbehavior. The long story made short is that, over time, there was a change of heart on the part of both husband and wife and an eventual reconciliation. No mortal could have orchestrated such a path, but the Lord could, and He did.

It is never for us to judge each other, which admittedly can be the most difficult of expectations at times. It is far more productive and helpful for us to remain ready, willing, and worthy so that the Lord can use us to bless each other's lives.

The reality is that repentance works, and because of the Atonement of Jesus Christ it is possible to repent of even serious sin. The stake president who presided at the disciplinary council of a friend, after indicating that my friend was to be excommunicated, said these simple but profound words: "You have left quite a trail of sin behind you. But you haven't done anything that you can't be completely forgiven of. And we, your brethren, are here to help you find your way back."

Stated simply, our Father wants His children back, and He will go to great lengths to help them—as evidenced, first and foremost, by the fact that He gave His Only Begotten Son, who in turn gave His life, that an Atonement would be made.

Repentance does indeed work. It is almost never too late, for any of us. A central message of the Book of Mormon is that through the Atonement of Jesus Christ we can be forgiven, cleansed from sin, washed white and purified. True repentance requires sincere faith, recognition of sin, godly sorrow, confession, restitution for sin, and forsaking or turning away from evil. There is nothing simple, easy, or painless about repentance, but because of the Atonement it is possible.

How do we know when repentance has taken effect? Consider another scriptural example. Though we tend to focus on the remarkable repentance and conversion of Alma the Younger, we sometimes overlook the fact that his father, Alma, also had a rocky start, as he himself explained: "I myself was caught in a snare, and did many things which were abominable in the sight of the Lord, which caused me sore repentance; Nevertheless, after much tribulation, the Lord did hear my cries, and did answer my prayers" (Mosiah 23:9–10).

From that time forward, Alma dedicated his life to the Lord, serving as an instrument in His hands the remainder of his days. And the result was stunning, for the time came when he heard this promise from God: "Thou art my servant; and I covenant with thee that thou shalt have eternal life" (Mosiah 26:20).

A sign of true repentance is abandonment of sin. Forsaking sin in the truest sense requires a comprehensive transformation of one's life, not merely the abandonment of a specified sin. The lives of both Almas illustrate this. But the important reality is simply that repentance does indeed work.

In some circumstances, a period of time is required for full restitution to be made and repentance to be complete. Very seldom does serious sin develop overnight, and equally seldom does restitution and repentance happen quickly.

But it is possible to change, to completely change. The Atonement of Jesus Christ is the Ultimate Agent for change. It is the only way by which we can really change and become new creatures (see Mosiah 27:26). If for some reason you don't believe such change is possible, may I suggest that you don't really believe in the gospel of Jesus Christ, and that your conversion to the gospel is not complete. The privilege of repenting and changing is at the very core of our doctrine. The Savior, if we will allow Him, will change our hearts, He will awaken us out of a deep sleep, He will awaken us to God—if we submit to His will and direction.

The Lord is merciful. He never stops working to redeem His children, and will go to extraordinary lengths to get them back. Long after we have given up on someone, the Lord is still working with that person and with those who can reach that person. Our challenge is to be in tune so that we can be instruments in the hands of the Lord to do all we can do to bring about the desired course of change. "For the Lord will be merciful unto all who call on his name" (Alma 9:17).

There is power in the Atonement to bring about complete and total change. There is power in the Atonement to help us repent of even the most serious offenses. There is power in the Atonement to make us completely new creatures, men and women "born of God, changed from their carnal and fallen state, to a state of righteousness, being redeemed of God, becoming his sons and daughters" (Mosiah 27:25).

I never cease to be amazed at the Lord's mercy, or at His patience. I have felt the changing, sanctifying power of Jesus Christ again and again, and I have seen the same magnificent effect in the lives of others. Jack was right: "The molding effect that the gospel has on people sure is a true power, if you'll let it be."

CHAPTER NINE

True Blue, Through and Through

You and I live in a world filled with pressure—pressure to accomplish, pressure to get ahead, pressure to be smarter than we are, pressure to conform, pressure to be popular. How can we stay true blue—to ourselves, to others, and to our Father and His Son?

NOT LONG AGO, when I was in a meeting with President Gordon B. Hinckley, he asked how work was going. Among other things, I described a difficult decision I had made that in retrospect I realized I had waited too long to make. "President, I just wish I were smarter," I confessed. Without missing a beat, he replied, "I wish you were smarter too." Then, after pausing for effect, he added, "I wish we were all smarter."

President Hinckley's statement is reminiscent of something that actor John Wayne is purported to have said: "Life is tough. But it's tougher when you're stupid."

Simply stated, there are advantages to being smart—smart in a variety of ways.

Typically, when we talk about intelligence, we resort to discussions about education or natural aptitude or I.Q. But in this context I invite you to think about virtue as being plain old smart—and in this application, I invite you to ponder a virtue that is not only smart but will have as much impact on your happiness, your peace of mind, and your ability to fulfill your life's mission as any virtue I can think of.

It is a virtue that will ultimately make you or break you. It will make or break you as a husband or wife, father or mother, brother or sister, colleague or friend or leader. It will make or break your career. It will make or break any relationship you enter into. Most significantly, it will make or break your efforts to achieve exaltation. For it will define your relationship with God the Father, His Son Jesus Christ, and the Holy Ghost.

This is a virtue that every man or woman of God must come to possess in increasing degrees. It is a virtue found in the truly great leaders of the world. It is a virtue found in every true follower of Jesus Christ.

It is the virtue of integrity.

We tend to define integrity as honesty. Without question, it includes that. But telling the truth is just the beginning of integrity.

President Joseph F. Smith called integrity "the cornerstone of character" (in *Conference Report*, April 4, 1897). President Gordon B. Hinckley spoke of integrity this way: "Men and women of integrity understand intrinsically that theirs is the precious right to hold their heads in the sunlight of truth, unashamed before anyone" (*Standing for Something*, 29).

An incident in the life of President Joseph F. Smith bears out this point. In the fall of 1857, the nineteen-year-old Joseph F. was returning from his mission in Hawaii, and in California he joined a wagon train. It was a volatile time for the Saints. Johnston's Army was marching toward Utah, and many had bitter feelings toward the Church. One evening several hoodlums rode into camp, cursing and threatening to hurt every Mormon they could find. Most in the wagon train hid in the brush down by a nearby creek. But the young Joseph F. thought to himself: "'Shall I run from these fellows? Why should I fear them?' With that he marched up with his arm full of wood to the campfire where one of the ruffians, still with his pistol in his hand, shouting and cursing about the 'Mormons,' in a loud voice said to Joseph F.: 'Are you a Mormon?' And the answer came straight, 'Yes, siree; dyed in the wool; true blue, through and through.' At that the ruffian grasped him by the hand and said: 'Well, you are the [blankety-blank] pleasantest man I ever met! Shake, young fellow, I am glad to see a man that stands up for his convictions'" (*Gospel Doctrine*, 518).

I love Joseph F. Smith's words: *true blue, through and through.*

For the purpose of better understanding the complete meaning of the word *integrity,* will you think of it as being *true: True Blue, Through and Through.* True to yourself, meaning who you are as a latter-day son or daughter of God, and who you are in the process of becoming. True to others, meaning that you do what you say you will do and that your word is good. And true to God, meaning that you practice what you preach and that you are doing what you covenanted to do here in mortality.

Living with integrity isn't necessarily easy, but, ironically, it is far easier than the alternative. Integrity engenders confidence and peace of mind, whereas breaching integrity always has painful consequences. A case in point:

I was raised on a large grain farm in Kansas, and on a farm you learn to drive as soon as you can see over the steering wheel *and* touch the pedals—preferably at the same time. For me, that was in the fourth grade. So, by the time I got my driver's license at fourteen, I was a seasoned veteran behind the wheel. Or so I thought.

That first June after getting my driver's license, I was expected to help with the harvest. My job was to drive a grain truck from the field to the elevators, ten miles away via country road. The trip to the elevator was a straight shot, except for one stop sign to cross a two-lane paved highway.

Now, it takes hundreds of yards to grind down through the gears and bring a fully loaded grain truck to a complete stop. It was a pain for a young girl. Each time I came to that stop sign, I couldn't help but think how much easier it would be if I didn't have to completely stop. It wasn't as though I *needed* to stop. There was rarely any traffic on that remote highway. And besides, Kansas is flat. You can stand on a tunafish can and see forever. So from the cab of the truck, I could see for miles. After indulging in these thoughts for a few days, I managed to rationalize that it was actually a good idea if I just slowed down but didn't completely stop.

I began to do that, and it did indeed make dealing with the stop sign *so much* easier. But then something curious began to happen. Before I knew it, not only was I not stopping, I wasn't doing much more than taking my foot off the pedal briefly, glancing both ways, and barreling across the highway. I did this day after day, including one afternoon when I again disregarded the stop sign, sped across the highway, and proceeded down the dirt country road toward our farm.

Now, I should point out that a heavy truck on a dirt road kicks up a lost of dust. That afternoon, after going five miles, I looked in the rearview mirror as I slowed to turn a corner and to my fourteen-year-old horror saw a white car with rotating red lights on top following me. I had never even *seen* a policeman out in the country, let alone talked to one. And after eating my dust for five miles, the officer was not all that cheerful. Then, when he saw how young I was, he was livid and demanded to talk with my parents. So with his red lights still gyrating (I mean, honestly, you would have thought my picture was on the post office wall), he followed me to our farm a mile away. Let's just say that the entire ordeal proved to be painful.

I learned three things that day: First, that with lightning speed, I went from complete observance to complete disregard of the law. Second, my demise started with a small crack in my integrity. The instant I talked myself into taking a small liberty with the law, I was on a slippery slide into full-scale disobedience. And third, there is actually no such thing as taking a small liberty with the law, or slightly breaking a law—whether a law of the land or a law of God—because even a slight breach of integrity opens the door for Satan.

Helaman's stripling warriors stand in stark contrast to my performance behind the wheel of the grain truck. They performed "every word of command with exactness" and "were true at all times in whatsoever thing they were entrusted" (Alma 57:21; 53:20). In other words, they kept their covenants with precision, and they could be counted on to do whatever they said they would do. They were true blue, through and through. They clearly understood that a half-hearted effort to keep the Sabbath day holy or to be morally clean or to tell the truth is no effort at all. Joseph Smith didn't declare that we *usually* believe in being "honest, true, chaste, benevolent, [and] virtuous" (Articles of Faith 1:13). On Mount Sinai the Lord didn't say, "Thou shalt *rarely* covet"; or "Thou shalt not steal *very often*"; or "Thou shalt only commit adultery a time or two." He said, "*Thou shalt not,*" clearly defining the line between integrity and infidelity, a line that when we cross we risk losing control of our thoughts, motives, and actions—just as I did in the grain truck.

Integrity is the foundational virtue upon which all other virtues are dependent. It is the first rung on the character ladder. Where there is integrity, other virtues will follow. Where there is no integrity, other virtues have no chance of developing.

Falsehood and breaches of integrity are as old as Cain and as recent as features in yesterday's news. Scan the front page of any newspaper, any day of the week, and you'll likely find an account of yet another CEO or public servant or even clergyman who has violated the trust of clients or constituents. Today there seem to be flagrant violations of integrity everywhere—the newsroom, the locker room, the board room, even the court room. We have endured so many outrageous national scandals that obscene abuses of power and money seem almost ho-hum. Leaders at the highest levels of government have committed unspeakable breaches of integrity—and then lied until forced to confess. Executives in one corporation after another have bilked investors out of billions. Others have lost fame and fortune simply because they lied.

Just prior to the 2000 presidential election, I was invited to address an East Coast professional organization on the topic of leadership. The gist of my message was that true leaders embodied certain virtues—with the key virtue being integrity—because a man or woman who can't be trusted can't really lead.

After the presentation, an accomplished businesswoman approached me. "You know," she said, "I've never thought about the connection between leadership and integrity. But I guess it really is impossible to lead people if they don't trust you."

Her reaction stunned me! Who wants to be led by a liar? Tell me, do you care if the professor who determines your grades is fair? Do you care if your banker is honest? Would you like to know that your surgeon didn't cheat his way through his residency? Do you care if the person you're dating or considering marrying tells you the truth about his life, his past, and his feelings about everything from the gospel to what kind of family he wants to have?

Of course you do, because it is not possible to develop a relationship, *any* relationship—whether between husband and wife, parent and child, teacher and student, or business and customer—with someone you can't trust. There is a reason adultery is referred to as "cheating," because it constitutes such a cruel breach of trust. And trust, which can be engendered only in an atmosphere of integrity, is the keystone that holds every organization together, whether it is a marriage or a family, a business or a nation, or even the kingdom of God.

Prophets and other righteous men and women have provided patterns to emulate. Consider Joseph, whose jealous, self-absorbed, rotten brothers sold him into Egypt and then lied about it. In stark contrast to his brothers, Joseph held fast to his integrity under the most trying of circumstances. Consider his words as he resisted the seductive advances of Potiphar's licentious wife: "Behold, my master . . . hath committed all that he hath to my hand; . . . neither hath he kept back any thing from me but thee, because thou art his wife: how then can I do this great wickedness, and sin against God?" (Genesis 39:9). Joseph was unwilling to betray either his friend or his God. He was true blue.

Job set an example of integrity for the ages. Even after losing his wealth, his health, and his family, he declared, "Till I die I will not remove mine integrity from me. My righteousness I hold fast, and will not let it go" (Job 27:5–6).

Then there was Saul, who went about destroying the Church—until his remarkable conversion. From that time forward, the Apostle Paul was faithful to his charge to "bear [the Lord's] name before the Gentiles, and kings, and the children of Israel" (Acts 9:15). He was stoned, persecuted, arrested, and bound in chains (see Acts 14:19; 21:33). Yet even before King Agrippa, he boldly declared the truth and was true to what he knew to be true.

The people of Anti-Nephi-Lehi, who underwent a dramatic conversion to the gospel, are also of interest. We know that those who converted to the Lord "never did fall away" (Alma 23:6). They were later described as being "distinguished for their zeal towards God" and as being "perfectly honest and upright in all things" (Alma 27:27). One can't help but notice the parallel between conversion and perfect honesty.

Prophets in our day have demonstrated similar valiance, beginning with the Prophet Joseph, whose vision of the Father and the Son consigned him to a lifelong crucible. He was mocked and persecuted, tarred and feathered, imprisoned for months at a time, and betrayed by trusted friends. Through it all he declared, "I have thought since, that I felt much like Paul, when he made his defense before King Agrippa, and related the account of the vision he had when he saw a light, and heard a voice; but still there were but few who believed him; some said he was dishonest, others said he was mad; and he was ridiculed and reviled. But all this did not destroy the reality of his vision. He had seen a vision, he knew he had, and all the persecution under heaven could not make it otherwise. . . . So it was with me. I had actually seen a light, and in the midst of that light I saw two Personages, and they did in reality speak to me; and though I was hated and persecuted for saying that I had seen a vision, yet it was true; . . . I had seen a vision; I knew it, and I knew that God knew it, and I could not deny it, neither dared I do it" (Joseph Smith–History 1:24–25). The Prophet Joseph never backed down. His was stunning integrity under stunning circumstances.

Joseph's successors have followed suit, including President Gordon B. Hinckley. After he was interviewed by Mike Wallace for *60 Minutes,* I spoke with Mr. Wallace about their interview. Of the many things Mr. Wallace praised President Hinckley for—his intellect, his sense of humor, his breadth of knowledge—he seemed most impressed with the fact that the prophet had done everything in connection with their interview that he had promised to do. When I later offered to show Mr. Wallace how I intended to quote him in President Hinckley's biography, he replied, "That's not necessary. You're a Mormon. I trust you." Do you really think this hard-hitting veteran journalist believes every member of the Church is trustworthy? Of course he doesn't! He is not that naive. But his statement was not a reflection of me or of us; it was a reflection of President Hinckley. Mr. Wallace was saying, in effect, "If you are associated with *that* man, then I assume that you, too, will do what you have said you will do." Mr. Wallace was commenting on a man who had once explained the fundamental secret of his character: "The course of our lives is not determined by great, awesome decisions," President Hinckley had said. "Our direction is set by the little day-to-day choices which chart the track on which we run" ("Watch the Switches in Your Life," 91).

The kind of trust Mike Wallace experienced with President Hinckley can only be earned one person at a time. This should encourage each of us to take a simple inventory: Do we do what we say we will do? Can we keep a confidence? Does our signature on a contract or a check or our temple recommend mean something? *Our word is who we are.* No wonder James the Apostle taught that "a double minded man is unstable in all his ways" (James 1:8).

Indeed, anything that lacks integrity is unstable, as any engineer will tell you. A bridge or skyscraper that has structural integrity does what it was built to do. It isn't necessarily perfect. It could have flaws. But, under stress and repeated use, it does what it was built to do. If, on the other hand, a structure does not have structural integrity, it will at some point fail, as was the case with the world's first jet airliner, the British-made de Havilland Comet.

When the Comet was introduced in 1949, the future seemed bright for jet travel—until three Comets disintegrated in flight, killing all aboard. The planes were grounded as puzzled engineers worked fever-ishly to understand why they had operated flawlessly at first, only to break apart later in midair. The engineers set up a fuselage in a large pool and pumped water in and out, simulating the effects of repeated cabin pressurization. At first, the experiment revealed nothing. But then it yielded a startling discovery. The repeated stress caused small cracks to form around the rectangular windows, cracks that soon widened into gaping holes. The planes could not withstand repeated pressure. They lacked structural integrity.

You and I live in a world *filled* with pressure—pressure to accom-plish, pressure to get ahead, pressure to be smarter than we are, pressure to conform, pressure to be popular. None of us are perfect. We all have flaws. How, then, under repeated pressure, can we avoid allowing small cracks in our integrity to form? How can we be sure that our character is structurally sound? How can we stay true blue—to ourselves, to others, and to our Father and His Son?

May I suggest seven things that will help us become men and women of integrity:

1. *Decide today, once and for all, that you will be worthy of trust*—the trust of family and friends, colleagues and business associates, and, most of all, the Lord. The more the Lord trusts you, the more knowledge and power He will give you.

Consider the exquisite promise the Lord made to Nephi, son of Helaman: "Blessed art thou, Nephi, . . . for I have beheld how thou hast with unwearyingness declared the word . . . unto this people. . . . Because thou hast done this with such unwearyingness, . . . I will make thee mighty in word and in deed, . . . yea, even that all things shall be done unto thee according to thy word, for thou shalt not ask that which is contrary to my will" (Helaman 10:4–5). Nephi had proven himself to the Lord. And because the Lord could trust him, He increased Nephi's access to His knowledge and power.

Trust is equally crucial to our relationships here. I have seen marriages crumble because husbands and wives couldn't trust each other's word or motives or faithfulness. I have seen families disintegrate because small cracks in a parent's integrity led to gaping emotional and spiritual holes. I have seen businesses collapse under the weight of executives who don't tell the truth and whose self-interests outweigh the greater good. Thirty years ago we saw a President of the United States removed from office because he lied and then lied about lying. And it almost happened again just a few years ago. I repeat what I said earlier: It is not possible to build a relationship with someone you can't trust. And nowhere is this more evident than in a marriage and family.

I know of a couple who struggled for years to build a satisfying relationship, but without success. The husband had learned to lie when the going got tough, and then to lie about lying. His wife, on the other hand, was so consumed with her desire to be liked and well thought of that she never discovered who she really was—rather than who she thought everyone expected her to be. She spent her time and money doing and buying things to be "seen of men and women." Both husband and wife were, in their own way, disingenuous. Neither was true to himself or herself, so their love could not grow.

During the two years I have served as the president of a company, I have gained new appreciation for how fundamental trust is to every relationship. Each time I have appointed an officer in our company, I have looked for individuals with the requisite skills and then posed an additional question: Can I trust this person's motives, judgment, and that he or she will tell me the truth? If I can answer yes to all three, the person is a candidate; if not, regardless of credentials, he or she is not.

The Holy Ghost is not able to inspire or endorse the words or actions of someone who is not true and who can't be trusted. So decide now, today, once and for all, that at all costs you will be a man or woman of integrity who can be trusted.

2. *Do what you say you will do.* In this regard, we ought to take a page out of the Nephites' (and sometimes, even the Lamanites') book. Oaths meant something to the Book of Mormon peoples. Their seriousness is demonstrated, for example, by the Lamanite leader Zerahemnah, who refused to swear a false oath to Moroni to surrender by pledging peace, even though he and his armies were surrounded (see Alma 44:1–20).

Why did Nephi trust that Laban's servant Zoram would not turn on him? Because Zoram swore an oath, which Nephi accepted as binding (see 1 Nephi 4:32–37).

If you say you'll do something, do it. If you make a promise, keep it. If you make a statement, do everything you can to make sure it's true.

3. *Make covenants and keep them.* This begins with keeping the covenants you made at baptism and in the House of the Lord, and then being precisely, completely true to those covenants.

But it also includes being fair and square with others. Here is a sample checklist:

- Do you do what you say you will do, or do you often make excuses for not coming through?
- Will you rationalize taking advantage of someone else if it is to *your* advantage?
- Do you give your best effort at work or just put in time?
- Do you pay a full tithe?
- Would you date your best friend's girlfriend behind his back?
- Are you honest with those you date, or are you leading someone on because no one better has come along and you don't want to sit home Friday night?
- What DVDs do you watch and web sites do you visit when you're alone?
- Are you honest and moral in the dark of night as well as broad daylight? Are you true to those who have trusted you with their love and confidence?
- Are you living worthy of the kind of man or woman you hope to marry, and of the children whom our Father will entrust to your care?

- If you are married, are you true to the man or woman you married and to the children you have had together?
- Are you completely, precisely true to the covenants you have made in the House of the Lord?
- When you partake of the sacrament, do you do so with a clean heart and hands?

Questions such as these simply invite a personal inventory. Now is the time to learn to be precisely honest. Now is the time to commit ourselves to lives of integrity. Everything we see around us convinces me that in future days we can expect to face dilemmas far more complex than the ones I have mentioned, but dilemmas that can almost always be resolved if we are fair and honest and true. So, as Amulek counseled the youth of his day, "learn wisdom . . . ; yea, learn . . . to keep the commandments of God" with exactness (Alma 37:35). Learn to be true to every covenant you make.

4. *Stand up for what you believe.* In fact, look for every opportunity to do so. There is no need to be showy or loud about it, and please don't ever criticize or judge others in the process. But relish every opportunity to stand for something, to be true to what you know is right.

Nine days after Heber J. Grant was born, his father died, and his widowed mother, Rachel, was left to carry on. She tried to support her young son by working as a seamstress and taking in boarders, but they remained desperately poor. Rachel's well-to-do brothers offered her a life of ease if she would renounce the Church. But she could not bring herself to turn her back on the gospel. Her prophet-son later spoke often about the dramatic impact her devotion had on him.

It is not possible to denounce who you are, or to live beneath who you are, and be happy. True happiness comes only when you are living up to who you are. King Benjamin understood this when he described the "happy state of those that keep the commandments of God. For . . . they are blessed in all things" (Mosiah 2:41).

If you want to feel *real* joy, keep the commandments and be true to who you are. It is actually easier to stand up for what you believe than to *not* do so. I was reminded of this last summer, when I was invited to speak about the family to a gathering of United Nations diplomats. I agonized over what to say to such a diverse group. In the end, I simply explained that my parents had taught me as a child that personal virtue was essential for a happy marriage and family, and that in my youth I had promised God that I would live a chaste life.

I then acknowledged that, though I had not yet had the chance to marry, I had kept my promise. "It hasn't always been easy to stay morally clean," I admitted. "It has required some self-discipline. But on balance, it has been far easier than the alternative. I have never spent one second worrying about an unwanted pregnancy or disease. I have never had cause to contemplate an abortion. I have never had a moment's anguish because a man used and then discarded me. And when I do marry, I will do so without regret. So you see," I concluded, "I believe a moral life is actually an easier and a happier life."

I worried about how such a sophisticated audience would respond to a message about virtue and abstinence, but to my surprise they leaped to their feet in applause—not because of me, but because the Spirit had borne witness of the truth of that simple message. The happiest people I know are those who have the integrity to stand up for what they believe.

5. *Expect your integrity to be challenged.* Metaphorically speaking, be

on the lookout for Potiphar's wife. She will show up again and again. Be ready to leave your cloak in her hand as Joseph did and flee again and again, because Satan won't tempt you just once. Moses had to resist Satan's temptations four times. He had to tell Satan to beat it four times before he finally left—and that was after the adversary ranted and raved and wailed and exposed Moses to the bitterness of hell (see Moses 1:19–22).

You too will have to tell Satan to beat it over and over again. Never forget that we are here on probation. We are here to be tested and to show, by our choices, whether we want to be part of the kingdom of God more than we want anything else. Satan knows this. So count on the fact that your integrity will be tested again and again. It will be tested in ways large and small. This is actually a blessing, for you don't really know what you believe until your beliefs are tested. You don't know if you're honest until your honesty is tested. You don't know if you really prize chastity until your virtue is tested. You don't know if you can be trusted—with someone's feelings, with money, with influence, with power—until your trust is tested. In every trial comes a moment of truth when you must decide what you really believe. As a Jewish proverb proclaims, "A man is not honest just because he has had no chance to steal" (Panati, *Words to Live By,* 22).

So count on tests of your integrity. Even welcome such tests. And know that every time we choose to be obedient, every time we make a tough but righteous choice, our integrity is fortified.

6. *Don't give up.* Developing integrity is a lifelong process. I am fifty years old, and I have to work at this every day. The older I get, and the more determined I become to keep the commandments with exactness, the more aware I am of how far I have to go, and the more often I find

myself seizing the opportunity to repent, to ask for forgiveness from the Lord and others, and then to try again. Daily repentance and precise obedience are crucial to increasing integrity. But then, that is the pattern of life. When you do something that introduces a crack into your integrity, if you are paying attention, the Spirit will let you know through His whisperings and the workings of your conscience that you have something to work on.

Recently while I was traveling a woman approached me and asked if I was the president of Deseret Book. When I nodded yes, she handed me a check and with emotion said, "Years ago I had a financial setback and could not pay a bill I owed your company. I have felt guilty ever since. Please take this so that my conscience can be clear again."

No one except the Savior will live a perfect life, and no one is perfected in a day. It takes time and sheer work to develop and refine our integrity. Heber J. Grant said it this way: "I know of no easy formula for success. Persist, persist, PERSIST; work, work, WORK—is what counts in the battle of life" (*Teachings of the Presidents of the Church: Heber J. Grant*, 36).

So learn to keep the commandments with exactness. Learn to delight in repenting and obeying. And don't give up.

7. *Covenant—or perhaps I should say, renew your covenant—with our Father and His Son to do what you came here to do.* Doing what we agreed to do premortally is the ultimate expression of our integrity.

As in all things, the Savior is the supreme example of perfectly fulfilling His foreordained mission. Premortally, when our Father outlined His plan and the need for a Redeemer, the Savior responded, "Here am I, send me" (Abraham 3:27).

He came, lived a sinless life, and at the appointed hour submitted to the agony of Gethsemane. He didn't do it for Himself; He was already a God. He did it for you and me.

Perhaps even the Savior didn't completely comprehend the depths to which He would be required to go, for there came that moment of unspeakable anguish when He pleaded, "Father, if thou be willing, remove this cup from me." But then, in the midst of His agony, He demonstrated supernal integrity by adding: "Nevertheless, not my will, but thine, be done" (Luke 22:42).

There was no ram in the thicket this time. The Son of God did what He was sent here to do. His was the ultimate honoring of a commitment. It was also an unparalleled example of something that should give each of us great courage, for at that sublime moment of submission, "there appeared an angel unto him from heaven, strengthening him" (Luke 22:43). Even the Savior wasn't required to complete His mission alone. And neither are we, if we too honor our eternal commitments and submit ourselves to God.

Later, on the cross, the Savior uttered seven final words: "It is finished, thy will is done" (JST, Matthew 27:50). From "Here am I, send me" to "It is finished, thy will is done," we have a pattern of perfect integrity.

We too made premortal commitments, among them surely being a willingness to come during this "eleventh hour" (see D&C 33:3). Surely we followed our Elder Brother's example. Perhaps we said something like this: "If you need someone who will have the courage and determination to face the world at its worst, here am I, send me. If you need husbands and wives who will be faithful to each other, raise their children in the admonition of the Lord, and defend the family, here am I, send me. If you need men and women who will see through the lies of the world about family and gender and intimacy, and who will never confuse being tolerant of others with tolerating sin, here am I, send me. If you need men and women who can think straight in a confused, twisted world, here am I, send me. If you need men and women who will be fearless in building the kingdom of God, please, here am I, send me."

President Boyd K. Packer said this: "The world is spiraling downward at an ever-quickening pace. I am sorry to tell you that it will not get better. I know of nothing in the history of the Church or in the history of the world to compare with our present circumstances. Nothing happened in Sodom and Gomorrah which exceeds the wickedness and depravity which surrounds us now. . . . The first line of defense—the home—is crumbling. Surely you can see what the adversary is about. We are now exactly where the prophets warned we would be" (BYU J. Reuben Clark Law Society Devotional, 28 February 2004).

I have no question that we are here now, that we were sent now, because we have everything it takes to deal with the world now. We were put through our paces premortally. That we are here *now* speaks to how well we did. We have it in us not only to withstand the pressures of the last days but to triumph over them.

Now, that doesn't mean we are living up to who we are. Typically we are in need of making some degree of course corrections. To help with this, I invite you to undergo the spring cleaning to end all spring cleanings by enrolling in Integrity 101. Let me outline the coursework. First, take an inventory of your integrity by asking yourself the kind of questions I listed earlier. Look for cracks that may have started to form. Be honest with yourself about your past dishonesties. Second, for the next thirty days take time every night to assess how you did that day. Were you true to yourself and to others? Were you true to God in every situation? See if this increased effort makes a difference in what you say, how you spend your time and money, the decisions you make, and what you repent of. See if it also makes a difference in how you feel about yourself and your life.

Finally, as you become more fully aware of your strengths and weaknesses, turn to the Savior more frequently and with increasing fervor. Thank our Father for the gift of His Son and the privilege of repenting. Express your deep desire to live with integrity. And then plead for help. The Savior has the power to help you change. He has the power to help you turn weakness into strength. He has the power to make you better than you have ever been.

I know that this is true, for I have felt His redeeming and enabling power again and again and again. May we come to be more true than we have ever been before—true to ourselves, true to others, and, most important, true to God, with whom we have made sacred covenants. May we be like the sons of Helaman—who were *strict* to remember God day in and day out, and who were true at all times to whatsoever thing with which they had been entrusted. May we be true blue, through and through.

We Were Born to Lead

CHAPTER TEN

Pure Leadership and
Prophets of God

*It's easy to spot Pure Leaders, because they help those
who follow them do more and see more and become more
than they could ever do or see or become on their own.*

E LIVE IN A FASCINATING ERA. It makes one wonder what we
were thinking when we volunteered—or were volunteered, and then agreed—to come now, during the
eleventh hour of the most dramatic dispensation in the earth's history.
Ours is a time filled with everything from the most spectacular scien-
tific and technological advances the world has ever known, to terrorism
and unspeakable acts of hate and violence and greed.

Taken all together, the times in which we live have cast a penetrating light on good versus evil, on what is important as opposed to what
is not, on the power of instantaneous, global communication for both
good and ill, on the differences between the philosophies of men and
the precepts of God, on the influence of pride and arrogance on people's

motives, on integrity and honesty, and on leadership—as defined by the world, and as defined by God.

Webster says leaders are guides, conductors, those who have commanding authority or influence.

Some years ago General Mark W. Clark spoke of leadership this way: "All nations seek it constantly because it is the key to greatness, sometimes to survival, the electric and elusive quality known as leadership. Where does juvenile delinquency begin? In leaderless families. Where do slums fester? In leaderless cities. Which armies fail? Which political parties fail? Poorly led ones. Contrary to the old saying that leaders are born not made, the art of leading can be taught and it can be mastered" (as quoted in *Thomas Jefferson Research Bulletin,* No. 23, December 1967).

A recent issue of *Fortune* magazine said this about leadership: "After years of losing ground to its dowdy cousin, Management, Leadership is back. And it's looking more vital than ever. Being a boss is not the same as being a leader. Bosses inherit subordinates. Leaders earn followers. But there is good news. People want to be led. Indeed, people are starved for it. For all the talk of empowerment and flattened hierarchies, leadership is something elemental. Primates choose leaders. Groups of 5-year-olds choose leaders. It's in our DNA" (*Fortune,* 12 November 2001).

When we think of leaders, we tend to focus on world leaders and heads of nations, chief executive officers, generals and admirals leading troops into battle, conquerors who build empires (be they conquering territory or industries), or even on-court or on-field sports heroes who lead their teams to victory, often against unfavorable odds.

But in reality, we are all leaders: As mothers and fathers, for the most crucial of all leadership takes place in the home, where parents have unmatched influence over the well-being and progression of their children. As community and Church leaders. As leaders of every imaginable kind of organization. As men and women willing to stand up for and try to live what they believe. As men and women willing to stand up for those who can't stand up for themselves. As men and women who will fight evil on every front. Every circumstance and situation mentioned—and many more—require solid, definable leadership.

Make no mistake about it, the most crucial leadership is not taking place on the battlefield, or in the boardroom, or even in the Oval Office—not that leadership there isn't crucial. Consider this statement from President Gordon B. Hinckley, made to the BYU student body: "You are good. But it is not enough just to be good. You must be good for something. The world must be a better place for your presence. And that good that is in you must be spread to others. I do not suppose that any of us here will be remembered a century from now. But in this world so filled with problems, so constantly threatened by dark and evil challenges, you can and must rise above mediocrity, above indifference. You can become involved and speak with a strong voice for that which is right. You cannot be indifferent to this great cause. You have accepted it. [This] is the cause of Christ. You cannot simply stand on the sidelines and watch the play between the forces of good and evil" ("Stand Up for Truth," 22–23).

President Hinckley was speaking about leadership, all kinds of leadership—moral leadership and leadership among our peers, leadership at work, leadership in times of peace and war, leadership in the home, leadership in the Church, leadership in our neighborhoods and cities and nations, leadership required just to stand up for what is right.

We of all people have a special responsibility to be leaders. We know why we're here, and where we have the potential of going. We know who we are, and who we have always been. And we know where to look for divine help, and how to seek that help. Elder Neal A. Maxwell said it this way: "By divine appointment, these are [our] days (Helaman 7:9), since 'all things must come to pass in their time' (D&C 64:32). Moreover, though we live in a failing world, we have not been sent here to fail. Recall the new star that announced the birth at Bethlehem? It was in its precise orbit long before it so shone. We are likewise placed in human orbits to illuminate. God is in the details!" ("Encircled in the Arms of His Love," 17–18).

Because we are all leaders, and because we were born to lead, we need to learn how. We need tutoring in the art of Pure Leadership—meaning, pure as in 100 percent the genuine article, and pure as in leadership patterned after the ways of God. The finest examples of Pure Leadership in every dispensation, including this one, are prophets of God.

It's easy to spot Pure Leaders, because they help those who follow them to *do* more and *see* more and *become* more than they could ever do or see or become on their own. In addition, Pure Leaders realize that leadership isn't about them, it's about the people they serve. It's about the people they are called to lead.

There are plenty of people in the world who have followers but who are not Pure Leaders. Satan got many to follow him premortally, but he wasn't a leader. He was a manipulator, a deceiver, a conqueror whose pride and ego drove him to conquer for the sake of conquest, and nothing else. Some who couldn't see through his guise chose to follow him, but he didn't lead them anywhere except to eternal destruction.

By contrast, the scriptures are replete with examples of men and women who have demonstrated stunning leadership—of families, of the Church, in battle, in doing what was right under the most adverse and even frightening conditions, in exile, and on and on. Consider just two: Joseph, who was sold into Egypt, and Captain Moroni.

Abandoned in a foreign land, separated from his family, Joseph knew the sting of loneliness, isolation, and betrayal. Nevertheless, he resisted the advances of Potiphar's wife and stood for morality when resisting immorality was not the politically correct thing to do. He was a visionary man whose faith enabled him to rise from the ashes to show great leadership, becoming first ruler of Potiphar's house and then ruler over all of Egypt. As such, and because of his acute spiritual capabilities, he helped prepare an entire people against a time of famine.

But we see perhaps his greatest leadership in the way he dealt with his shiftless, conniving brothers. After all they had done to him, when they came to Egypt seeking relief from the drought, he sent them home to retrieve their father. Instead of scolding or lecturing them, instead of treating them as though they couldn't be trusted, instead of consigning them to some kind of bondage, he counseled them simply, "See that ye fall not out by the way" (Genesis 45:24).

Joseph showed leadership in forgiving his brothers of their horrendous misdeed, in rising above homesickness and resentment, in cultivating an attitude of faith in the Lord, and even in offering gentle counsel as his brothers left for home.

Captain Moroni also demonstrated remarkable leadership in a remarkable time when the bloodthirsty Lamanites far outnumbered the Nephites. Spiritually, he prepared the minds of the people to be faithful to God and to be "firm in the faith of Christ" (Alma 48:13). Temporally, he urged them to build forts and walls and large mounds of dirt. He placed the greatest number of men in the weakest fortifications. Even when the Lamanites withdrew for a time, Moroni did not stop making preparations. He was constantly fortifying the line between his people and the enemy.

At a crucial time he planted a Title of Liberty and marched forward, inviting all who would stand up and be counted to follow. And when the Nephites were about to shrink from fear of the larger, more ferocious Lamanite army, Moroni rallied them with "thoughts of their lands, their liberty, yea, their freedom from bondage." The result was that they were able to stand "against the Lamanites with power" (Alma 43:48, 50).

The summary statement about his leadership is classic: "If all men had been, . . . and ever would be, like unto Moroni, behold, the very powers of hell would have been shaken forever; yea, the devil would never have power over the hearts of the children of men" (Alma 48:17).

The same could be said of all prophets of God, who constitute the greatest Pure Leaders this world has ever seen. There is much we can learn about the essential qualities of a Pure Leader by identifying the qualities and virtues exemplified by these divinely chosen men—qualities and virtues that we must cultivate if we wish to be successful in the leadership we are trying to provide, wherever that may be. Consider the following:

A PURE LEADER IS HUMBLE

Pure Leaders understand three things clearly: first, that any skill, talent, or ability they have, along with their opportunity to serve, comes from God; second, that being a leader isn't about them, but about those they lead; and third, that leadership is not about elevating self, but about lifting others. Elder B. H. Roberts taught that the "highest form of leadership" is in "lifting others to excellence" (Madsen, *Defender of the Faith*, 90).

President Hinckley has often been heard to say, "Adulation is poison. Adulation has ruined too many good men and women" (Dew, *Go Forward with Faith*, ix). Indeed, despite the significant contributions he has made to the growth and development of the Church for nearly five decades, and the prominence and accolades that have accompanied his efforts, President Hinckley has managed to escape the trap of believing he is the one who has done it all.

During an interview with the producer of CBS's *60 Minutes*, Bob Anderson, one interchange went as follows:

Anderson: "You have been described as humorous and serious."

President Hinckley: "I am just a little fella trying to get along in the big leagues."

Anderson: "You seem genuinely humble in your position."

President Hinckley: "I feel that way. This Church isn't my Church. This is the Lord's Church. It carries His name. I am His servant. I want to do what He wants and I want to do it the best way I possibly can. Believe me, it is an awesome responsibility for [a man my age], who maybe ought to have been turned out to pasture 20 years ago."

In a meeting of General Authorities, President Hinckley said this: "I just cannot get over the tremendous responsibility we have. There has been laid upon us as people of ordinary talents the work of carrying the gospel of Jesus Christ to all the world. I just speak of myself and wonder if I should be doing a little more."

Leadership is not about subservience, or caste, or class. It is not about elevating oneself above others. It is not about the roar of the crowd. It is about lifting others. One sure way to identify Pure Leaders is that they are humble enough to accept responsibility for mistakes, but always quick to place the credit for their success where it belongs—with those who have helped them, and particularly with the Lord. As President Hinckley has said, "We cannot afford to be arrogant. We should walk with the knowledge that we will need help every step of the way" (*Standing for Something*, 89).

A PURE LEADER IS FIERCELY DEVOTED
TO A RIGHTEOUS CAUSE

Not only are Pure Leaders fiercely devoted to righteous causes but, in addition, their ambition is not for themselves, but for the people or the institutions or the causes they represent. There are countless examples of this among ancient and modern-day prophets.

Again, consider Captain Moroni. During the time he commanded the Nephite armies, "never had the Lamanites been known to fight with such exceedingly great strength and courage. Nevertheless, the Nephites were inspired by a better cause, for they were not fighting for monarchy nor power but they were fighting for their homes and their liberties, their wives and their children, and their all, yea, for their rites of worship and their church." (Alma 43:43–45).

Pure Leaders are devoted to righteous causes they believe in and are completely committed to. At one point, when President Hinckley's schedule was heavy and unrelenting, Sister Hinckley asked if he really needed to push himself so hard. He responded, "But don't you understand, I *love* this work!"

A PURE LEADER HAS FAITH IN GOD

Not only do Pure Leaders always acknowledge that their strength and ability comes from God, they truly believe He will help them.

When President Ezra Taft Benson was serving as Secretary of Agriculture, he often found himself at the center of a media maelstrom. He was working nearly around the clock, getting attacked regularly in the press, and still handling some assignments as a member of the Quorum of the Twelve. One day a young associate in the Department of Agriculture, who had watched him handle suffocating stress and an exhausting schedule with grace and graciousness again and again, asked him how he managed it all. President Benson's response was simple: "I work as hard as I can. I try to be obedient so the Lord knows I'm serious about Him. And then I trust the Lord to make up the difference" (from personal interview).

Not long after missionary work was inaugurated in the Philippines in 1961, President and Sister Hinckley escorted four missionaries to Manila to help them find housing and get them established as the first missionaries in that tropical land. As the Hinckleys prepared to leave, Sister Hinckley's maternal instincts took over and she said to her husband, in so many words, "You're not going to leave those four boys here by themselves, are you?" "They're not alone," he responded. "The Lord is with them." When the Hinckleys returned six months later to check on the missionaries, a small branch was thriving—all because of the efforts of "those four boys."

In short, President Hinckley has stated: "I . . . believe that God will always make a way where there is no way. I believe that if we will walk in obedience to the commandments of God, if we will follow the counsel of the priesthood, he will open a way even where there appears to be no way" ("If Ye Be Willing and Obedient," 2).

A PURE LEADER IS SOMEONE YOU CAN TRUST

In other words, a Pure Leader has integrity. Practically speaking, you can trust Pure Leaders because they tell the truth, they do what they say they will do, and they try to live what they believe.

A study examining those who have been financially successful revealed that, in the world of business, "being honest with people" is the number-one factor leading to success: "Unfortunately, today's headlines are full of reports about people in high places who lack integrity. Even President Bill Clinton suggested that his deceptive acts be placed in a 'box score' context, implying that his overall batting average as president was good to terrific. Most economically successful people don't believe that integrity, or lack of it, can be averaged into one's overall grade point average. . . . Integrity is a different part of life's curriculum. It is a pass/fail course" (Stanley, *The Millionaire Mind*, 54).

Being honest and having integrity go far beyond just telling the truth. They have everything to do with the issue of living what we believe. But George Washington lamented in a 1779 letter to a friend that "few men have the virtue to withstand the highest bidder" (Panati, *Words to Live By*, 280). Without exception, prophets have resisted the highest bidder in exchange for living true to their beliefs and their word.

While serving as Secretary of Agriculture, President Ezra Taft Benson got raked over the coals in one congressional hearing and by one reporter after another. But over time, he won the respect of even those who opposed his philosophies. A reporter for the *New York Times* surmised that the reason for President Benson's success was his integrity: "He acts like a man whose conscience is always clear—his testimony today will be the same next week or the week after or a year from now. He doesn't have to remember what he said to an opposition Senator at their last meeting. This is a built-in ulcer-saving device not always found in Washington." And in an introduction at the National Press Club, this was said of him: "Despite the heat Secretary Benson has taken, he has stood his ground. Surely it can be said he is a man of great integrity. And he has guts."

During his grueling eight years in the President's Cabinet, President Benson was often heard to say: "I feel it is always good strategy to stand up for the right, even when it is unpopular. Perhaps I should say, especially when it is unpopular" (Dew, *Ezra Taft Benson: A Biography*, 373).

A PURE LEADER IS WILLING TO WORK

President Hinckley has often said, "The only way I know to get anything done is to get on my knees and plead for help and then get on my feet and go to work." And go to work he has, his entire life. One letter from Sister Hinckley to her children described the life her husband was leading: "This sounds repetitious, but I have never known Dad to be so busy. He is trying to keep so many balls in the air he does not do justice to anything and it is frustrating for him. He said last night he is weary of sitting in meeting after meeting trying to be smarter than he is. At a time when most men retire he seems to be stretching himself further and further" (Letter to family, 2 March 1980).

During a mission tour in Korea in the 1960s, he spoke one evening in a cold building. As he was speaking, a coal stove blew apart and spewed a huge cloud of coal dust over him and the congregation. But he just kept on teaching.

In the press conference held just prior to the dedication of the Nauvoo Temple, President Hinckley admitted, "We're in a hurry. We have a lot of work to do." Indeed, the titles of his addresses through the years are revealing—"We Have a Work to Do," "Rise to a Larger Vision of the Work," and "Let Us Move This Work Forward"—as were his words in his first general conference as President of the Church: "We have work to do, you and I, so very much of it. Let us roll up our sleeves and get at it, with a new commitment, putting our trust in the Lord. We can do better than we have ever done before" ("We Have a Work to Do," 88).

A PURE LEADER IS OPTIMISTIC

Because of their faith and their penchant for doing their part through hard work, Pure Leaders are optimistic about the future as well as about the people they lead.

Again, President Hinckley epitomizes this quality. One of his classic and oft-quoted phrases is, "Things will work out." He's realistic, but not a doomsayer. He says today's youth are the best this world has ever seen. When critics take potshots at the Church, he calmly explains that they might have their moment in the sun but will then fade away, while the spark that was kindled in Palmyra will march boldly on. He has said that one of his few regrets is that he won't be around to see everything that is going to happen.

When a mission president in Korea wrote to a young Elder Hinckley, telling him the sad tale of monsoon rains that sent a wall of water cascading down upon the mission home, Elder Hinckley wrote the following in return: "We have your letter of July 22, 1966, with reference to the flood, which engulfed the mission home property. Needless to say this was a frightening experience and doubtless a costly one. You may be interested to know that the night before the London Temple was dedicated we had a flood of serious proportions there. I stood in water to my waist with others bailing it out. This went on for hours. I only want to suggest that your experience is not peculiar to Korea. Noah had a worse time. Sincerely, your brother" (Dew, *Go Forward with Faith*, 287).

Pure Leaders combine two seemingly opposite messages. This has been referred to as the "Churchill paradox." On one hand, he promised "blood, toil, tears, and sweat," but on the other hand he assured all of England that they would prevail "however long and hard the road may be."

Prophets almost always do the same. President Ezra Taft Benson frequently included in many of his addresses the words, "We can do it. I know we can."

A PURE LEADER BELIEVES IN AND CARES ABOUT PEOPLE

Pure leaders love the people they lead, believe in the people they lead, champion and build up the people they lead, and are determined to help them be more and do more than they could ever be or do on their own. Seeing others progress is the motive of Pure Leaders. It is what drives them.

Because of this, pure leaders are inclusive rather than exclusive. Whereas the world thrives on competitions that crown one winner while excluding (and sometimes humiliating) the others, the Lord's pattern is completely opposite. The only exclusivity with the Lord is based upon obedience and righteousness, for He has made it abundantly clear

that we may all inherit everything He has, if we will qualify: "If ye seek
the riches which it is the will of the Father to give unto you, ye shall be
the richest of all people, for ye shall have the riches of eternity" (D&C
38:39).

When President Hinckley was assigned as a young General
Authority to supervise the work in Asia in the 1960s, the Church was
in its infancy there. The first Korean man to be called to serve as a
General Authority, Elder Han In Sang, remembered those early days
when President Hinckley would travel from city to city in Korea, teaching and encouraging the people. "Again and again he told us, You are
as capable as any men and women on earth. He told us we were important and that we could be leaders. No one had ever said that to us
before. We didn't believe in ourselves, but he did" (interview with Han
In Sang, 31 March 1995).

In Japan during that same time, in meeting after meeting, President
Hinckley sat on the *tatami* mats with the people and taught them, sometimes one-on-one. His emphasis today on retention of converts is not
new. It began years ago, as he gained a love and respect for the people
he served.

Pure Leaders love the people they serve.

A PURE LEADER COMMUNICATES

A Pure Leader understands that, for good or ill, the power of communication is profound. Consider Captain Moroni's power of persuasion
as contrasted with that of Korihor, who for a time flattered the people
and used his powers of expression to deceive and destroy all who suc-
cumbed to his connivery and cunning. Consider the differences between
Jacob and Sherem. Again, Sherem relied upon the power of language and

his flair for flattery and persuasion, while Jacob drew upon the power of God.

A Pure Leader understands that you can't build relationships if you don't communicate. You can't really come to love someone if there isn't some kind of communication. You can't solve problems if you don't or won't communicate. You can't empathize or express love if you don't or won't communicate. You can't inspire or motivate if you can't communicate. In short, your influence is severely diminished if you can't or won't communicate.

Prophets from Nephi and the Brother of Jared to the Prophet Joseph to President Gordon B. Hinckley have been able and willing to draw upon the powers of heaven to expand their own abilities so that they could communicate effectively and persuasively.

A PURE LEADER HAS VISION

Pure Leaders can imagine things that don't yet exist. They tend to have respect and reverence for the past, but they also welcome and are optimistic about the future. It is difficult for us to put in context and thus fully appreciate some of the statements of the Prophet Joseph and Brigham Young. But in those earliest days, when mobs raged and the Church was under attack in nearly every quarter; when the Saints were called to sacrifice even their own lives in some circumstances; and when the faithful were leaving home after home and city after city, the first two Presidents of the Church repeatedly spoke about how the work of establishing the kingdom of God would spread across the world, to every nation, kindred, tongue, and people. They repeatedly affirmed that nothing would stop the work of the Lord.

Consider these remarkable and visionary words from the Prophet

Joseph, written in 1842 when he was essentially under siege: "No unhallowed hand can stop the work from progressing; persecutions may rage, mobs may combine, armies may assemble, calumny may defame, but the truth of God will go forth boldly, nobly, and independent, till it has penetrated every continent, visited every clime, swept every country, and sounded in every ear, till the purposes of God shall be accomplished, and the Great Jehovah shall say the work is done" (*History of the Church*, 4:540). Imagine that kind of vision so early in the Church's history!

Brigham demonstrated the same. The courage and vision required to lead the Saints out of Nauvoo and into the uncharted West, after they had suffered the loss of their prophet-leader, cannot possibly be measured. As though the challenge of leading the Saints into the Salt Lake Valley weren't enough, once there he immediately began a program of colonization that led to the development of cities throughout the West, and particularly throughout the territory of Deseret. His was a remarkable vision and tenacity.

Since those earliest days, with each successive President of the Church, the pioneering has continued. In recent years, under the direction of President Hinckley, the quorums of Seventy have been expanded, the number of temples around the world dramatically increased, and progressive media efforts employed to help bring the Church out of obscurity, to name just a few recent advancements.

Pure Leaders have full respect for the foundation laid by those who have gone before. They understand clearly that we all stand on the shoulders of those who preceded us. But, drawing upon that realization, they then imagine things that don't presently exist and press forward to build upon that foundation.

A PURE LEADER HAS THE COURAGE TO STAND ALONE

Without exception, Pure Leaders are called to stand by their convictions, and at times they have to stand alone.

Consider Adam and Eve, and the isolation and bewilderment they must have felt when they were expelled from the Garden. What stunning leadership! Or Abraham, when he was called to take his miracle son Isaac to Mount Moriah and there offer him as a sacrifice to the Lord. Or Noah, who built an ark on dry ground amid the jeers of those who thought he was crazy. Or Nephi, who was attacked again and again by his jealous brothers but who stood firm through it all. Or Moroni. There are few passages of scripture as sobering and tender as those written by Moroni, when he alone remained: "I had supposed not to have written more, but I have not as yet perished; and I make not myself known to the Lamanites lest they should destroy me. And because of their hatred they put to death every Nephite that will not deny the Christ. And I, Moroni, will not deny the Christ; wherefore, I wander whithersoever I can for the safety of mine own life" (Moroni 1:1–3). What loneliness he must have experienced, and yet he stood firm.

Try for a moment to imagine the loneliness of Joseph Smith, who just before Carthage said, "If my life is of no value to my friends it is of none to myself" (*History of the Church*, 6:549). Or Brigham Young, after the martyrdom. He'd just lost his best friend, who was also the Prophet, and now it was left to him to lead this beleaguered band of Saints West.

It is no different today, for any of us. More than thirty years ago, in a classic address entitled "The Loneliness of Leadership," President Hinckley said this: "[A] position of leadership was imposed upon us by the God of heaven. When the declaration was made concerning the only true and living Church upon the face of the earth, we were immediately put in a position of loneliness, the loneliness of leadership from which we cannot shrink nor run away and which we must face up to with boldness and courage and ability."

As he pointed out: "The price of leadership is loneliness. The price of adherence to conscience is loneliness. The price of adherence to principle is loneliness. I think it is inescapable. . . . But a man . . . has to live with his convictions. . . . Unless he does so, he is miserable—dreadfully miserable" (BYU Devotional, 4 November 1969).

The epitome, of course, of any of these virtues, and certainly the epitome of having the courage to stand alone, is Jesus Christ. There is no greater example of loneliness or demonstration of courage and leadership. "The foxes have holes," he said, "and the birds of the air have nests; but the Son of man hath not where to lay his head" (Matthew 8:20).

He endured Gethsemane alone. He endured the cross alone. He did not do it for Himself. He was already a God. He did it for us. He was and is the consummate, ultimate example of a Pure Leader.

We are all leaders. We were born to lead, in circumstances large and small, highly visible and obscure, in all the nations of the earth. If we are going to fulfill our foreordained assignments, we need to learn how to step forward, to help others do more and become more than they could ever do or become on their own, and then to lead out in whatever circumstances we find ourselves.

Prophets constitute, individually and collectively, the greatest group of Pure Leaders this world has ever known. They are not perfect men, but they are men called, chosen, and prepared by God to lead His people. He Himself has designed and put them through a divine tutorial to ready them for their sacred and holy calling. They have been taught how to lead by the Master Himself, and in turn, many of them have mastered the essence of Pure Leadership.

As in all things, when it comes to learning how to lead, in prophets of God we find models we may safely and enthusiastically emulate.

CHAPTER ELEVEN

Defenders of the Family

*As women who care about our families in particular and about the family
in general, as mothers and wives, grandmothers and sisters and aunts, we no
longer have the luxury of standing by and watching what is happening
all around us. It is time to stand up and be counted.*

S A JOURNALIST FOR THE *Saturday Evening Post* in Europe during
the 1930s, Dorothy Thompson witnessed Hitler's rise to
power. During an address at a convention in Toronto on May 2,
1941, she said this: "Before this epoch is over, every living human being
will have chosen. Every living human being will have lined up with
Hitler or against him. Every living human being will either have
opposed this onslaught or supported it. For if he tries to make no
choice, that in itself will be a choice. If he takes no side, he is on Hitler's
side. If he does not act, that is an act—for Hitler" (Torricelli and Carroll,
eds., *In Our Own Words*, 130).

Dorothy Thompson's statement interests me not because of the sentiment she expresses about Hitler (whose atrocities are not related or

germane to this discussion), but because she expressed a true principle in a way that is easy to grasp. When it comes to anyone or anything that attempts to destroy society or undermine principles or values, if we stand by and watch as the destruction takes place, if we take no stand for what is right, then we are, in essence, supporting the other side. With that concept in mind, let me use Dorothy Thompson's approach, but change her words to raise an issue of paramount importance:

"Before this era is over, every living human being will have chosen. Every living human being will have lined up in support of the family as we know it and as God intended it, or against it. Every living human being will either have opposed the onslaught against the family or supported it. For if we make no choice, that in itself will be a choice. If we do not act in behalf of the family, that itself will be an act in opposition to the family."

The family is under attack from all corners. Little by little, step by step, we have moved into dangerous territory with respect to the definition and protection of marriage and the natural and traditional family—meaning mother, father, and children—as the most important and significant unit of society. Things have progressed—or digressed and deteriorated—so far that we even see legal protections being advanced in behalf of various kinds of groupings of individuals, with this transition viewed by many commentators as not only positive but essential for an "open-minded" society.

Here are just a few examples of what we see happening all around us:

• Recent numbers from the U.S. Census Bureau show that married-couple households have slipped from nearly 80 percent in the 1950s to 50.7 percent today. This means that in the United States, the 86 million single adults could soon characterize the new majority. This tsunami-like societal shift is occurring because more people are delaying marriage, cohabiting outside the bonds of marriage, forming same-sex partnerships, living longer, and remarrying less. To quote the sentiment advanced recently in a popular national magazine, "What many once thought of as the fringe is becoming the new normal. Families consisting of breadwinner dads and stay-at-home moms now account for just one-tenth of all households. Married couples with kids, which made up nearly every residence a century ago, now total just 25%" (*Business Week*, 20 October 2003).

- Attitudes about marriage are changing in other ways as well. According to research conducted at the University of Michigan, more than half of female high school seniors say they believe having a child out of wedlock is okay. And 40 percent of women in their twenties say they would consider having a baby on their own if they reach their thirties and aren't married (see *Business Week*, 20 October 2003).

- A Colorado daily newspaper came out in defense of polyamory, which allows men who wish to have physical relationships with several women at a time to do so, as opposed to marrying any one of them. It was defined as "responsible non-monogamy," because some men just don't want relationships to be limited to two people. In other words, those promoting polyamory don't want to be limited by something as archaic as marriage (see *Boulder Daily Camera*, 5 July 2003).

- The Texas Supreme Court legalized sodomy.

- Officials from California to Boston have performed gay marriages, with the Massachusetts Supreme Court ruling in favor of legalizing gay marriage.

- As of mid-July 2004, Congress had refused to put forward for vote an amendment limiting the definition of marriage to a union between a man and a woman.

And on it goes.

On January 2, 2000, a major news program presented a segment predicting trends for the 21st century. Among other trends noted, they prophesied a redefinition of the family, concluding with the words, "At the end of this century, the family won't look like it does now" (*Today*, 2 January 2000). Unfortunately, at our current rate, it won't take nearly that long. Threats to the family are accelerating and occurring at an alarming rate.

How serious is this? Prophets, seers, and revelators both ancient and modern have spoken repeatedly in defense of the family unit. One of the very first things Adam was taught in the Garden was that it was not good for man to be alone, and a help meet was made for him. "And of the rib which the Gods had taken from man, formed they a woman, and brought her unto the man. And Adam said: This was bone of my bones, and flesh of my flesh; now she shall be called Woman, because she was taken out of man; Therefore shall a man leave his father and his mother, and shall cleave unto his wife" (Abraham 5:16–18). So from earliest days, God set forth and outlined the divine pattern as it relates to men and women, marriage, and the family.

More recently, President Gordon B. Hinckley declared: "The family is falling apart all over the world. The old ties that bound together father and mother and children are breaking everywhere. . . . Can we not do better? Of course, we can. It is selfishness that brings about most of these tragedies. . . . As I look to the future, I see little to feel enthusiastic about concerning the family in America and across the world. . . . [The situation will] get worse unless there is an underlying acknowledgment, yes, a strong and fervent conviction, concerning the fact that the family is an instrument of the Almighty. It is His creation. It is also the basic unit of society" ("Look to the Future," 69).

A year later, President Hinckley picked up the theme again: "I believe our problems, almost every one, arise out of the homes of the people. If there is to be reformation, if there is to be a change, if there is to be a return to old and sacred values, it must begin in the home. It is here that truth is learned, that integrity is cultivated, that self-discipline is instilled, and that love is nurtured. It is in the home that we learn the values by which we guide our lives. That home may be ever so simple . . . but with a good father and a good mother, it can become a place of wondrous upbringing. . . . It is broken homes that lead to a breakup in society" ("Walking in the Light of the Lord," 99–100).

Study after study has produced volumes of statistics verifying President Hinckley's point—that strong marriages and strong homes are one of the republic's greatest stabilizers. Voluminous amounts of data demonstrate a host of things: (1) that those who get married and stay married are happier, more healthy, earn more, are less likely to become addicted to something, are less prone to illness, and are less likely to live in poverty; (2) that the ideal environment for a child is living with a mother and father who love each other. Please do not misunderstand, this is not to suggest that single parents can't and don't raise spectacular children, because they can and do. It is simply to say that the studies show that the most ideal environment for any child is with two parents, a mother and a father; (3) that children who don't live with both parents are more likely to grow up poor, have problems in school, have more health and emotional problems, and get into trouble with the law; (4) that children from divorced homes are more likely to get divorced themselves; (5) that children whose parents divorce are more likely to skip school, get drunk, hurt someone enough to need a doctor, steal, and lie. On the other hand, data shows that teenagers whose parents worship together regularly are far less likely to engage in premarital sex (see Wilkins, "The Social Role of the Family"; *Business Week*, 20 October 2003, 106–16; Hinckley, *Standing for Something*, 147; *National Longitudinal Survey of Youth*).

I am neither a family researcher nor a sociologist, and don't pretend to be. But the pile of family research available from many independent institutions seems undeniable and conclusive. Stable marriages and stable families result in stable people. And stable people create stable societies. So individuals, groups, organizations, or philosophies that seek to undermine the sanctity and stability of the family as God defined it—between a man and woman, raising children in their home—ought to concern every one of us.

Nearly twenty-five years ago, President Spencer W. Kimball made a statement that was clearly prophetic: "The time will come when only those who believe deeply and actively in the family will be able to preserve their families in the midst of the gathering evil around us" (in *Conference Report*, October 1980, 3).

It looks as though that time has come. For if I were Satan and wanted to thoroughly obliterate society, I would try to undermine and eventually destroy the family. And I would do it in a number of ways: I would attempt to confuse men and women about the divine nature of their distinctive roles. I would try to deceive and distract and discourage women, such that they no longer feel joy in womanhood and motherhood. I would try to frustrate the plan of salvation by doing anything possible to interrupt the divine pattern that brings children to the earth—hence today's fascination with everything from abortion to homosexuality. I would attempt to redefine the family so that it applies essentially to any group of people who choose to define themselves as such. And on and on.

Said Elder L. Tom Perry: "It is becoming increasingly evident that Satan is working overtime to enslave the souls of men. His main target is the fundamental unit of society—the family. During the past few decades, Satan has waged a vigorous campaign to belittle and demean this basic and most important of all organizations. . . . Surely we have learned by now, from the experience over centuries, that the basic family provides the most stable and secure foundation for society and is fundamental to the preparation of young people for their future responsibilities. We should have learned by now that alternate styles of family formations have not worked and never will work" ("Fatherhood, An Eternal Calling," 69–70).

It has now been nearly ten years since the First Presidency and Council of the Twelve responded to the corrosive elements attacking the family by issuing "The Family: A Proclamation to the World," in which they clearly enumerated fundamental, God-given principles about this precious unit. This inspired document teaches that marriage between a man and a woman is ordained of God and that the family is ordained of God and is central to our Creator's plan for the eternal destiny of His children; that we are spirit sons and daughters of God created in the image of God; that we as God's children have been commanded to multiply and replenish the earth, but that the sacred powers of creation are to be employed exclusively between husband and wife; that children deserve to be born to two parents who are married to each other and who will care for them; that fathers and mothers are equal partners; and that the family is the fundamental unit of society (see "The Family: A Proclamation to the World").

The Proclamation also clearly indicates that, by divine design, fathers are to preside over their families while mothers are primarily responsible for the nurture of their children. It is about the influence women, and particularly mothers, in the family can have that this chapter focuses. Please do not interpret this choice of emphasis as being neglectful or disrespectful of men and fathers and their essential and divinely appointed role in the family. Nothing could be further from the truth. I love men! I love working with men. I love the men in my family and have profound respect for the principled men with whom I work and interact. But because there has historically been a tendency to overlook the unique but stunning influence of women, it seems appropriate to focus on how visibly women's influence is demonstrated in the home and family.

Thus, the emphasis in the rest of this chapter is simply an enthusiastic show of support for the distinctive and unparalleled impact women have in and on the family, and therefore in and on society. For as President Gordon B. Hinckley declared to the women of the Church, "If anyone can change the dismal situation in which we are sliding, it is you. Rise up, O women of Zion, rise to the great challenge which faces you. Stand above the sleaze and the filth and the temptation which is all about you." After then detailing some of society's ills, he added, "I do not hesitate to say that you who are mothers can do more than any other group to change this situation. All of these problems find their root in the homes of the people. . . . My beloved sisters, my message to you, my challenge to you, my prayer is that you will rededicate yourselves to the strengthening of your homes" ("Walking in the Light of the Lord," 99–100).

Truly, as women who care about our families in particular and about the family in general, as mothers and wives, grandmothers and sisters and aunts, we no longer have the luxury of standing by and watching what is happening all around us. It is time to stand up and be counted. The time has come to stand up, to defend, and to protect the family.

President Kimball stated that "leadership is the ability to encourage the best efforts of others in working toward a desirable goal" (*Teachings of Spencer W. Kimball,* 322). Put in that context, women are among the most influential leaders in the world—beginning with mothers, but including also grandmothers, sisters, wives, friends, daughters, colleagues, and confidantes. President Joseph F. Smith seemed to agree. Said he: "There are people fond of saying that women are the weaker vessels. I don't believe it. Physically, they may be; but spiritually, morally, . . . and in faith, what man can match a woman who is really convinced?" (as quoted in Widtsoe, *Priesthood and Church Government,* 86).

Periodically the Gallup organization asks respondents in the United States, "What is the most important problem facing the country?" When that question was posed in 1999, for the first time in history concerns over ethics, morality, and family decline topped the list. One in six adults believed these concerns to be more pressing than those dealing with violence and the economy (see *Emerging Trends,* 102). Women are vital to building character and instilling morals and values in the family. Indeed, women, beginning with mothers—but not limited to mothers— are uniquely positioned at the crossroads where they may, day in and day out, teach and model values and virtues to the rising generation.

Thomas Jefferson's daughters, Martha and Mary, were ten and four years of age when their mother died. Throughout his daughters' lives, Jefferson tended to rely on Martha to help him teach and raise Mary. On one occasion he told his eldest daughter: "Teach [Mary] above all things to be good: because without that we can be neither valued by others or ourselves" (Bennett, *Spirit of America*, 223).

Several years ago, not long after the Columbine High School shooting disaster in Colorado, I attended a luncheon honoring Mrs. Jehan Sadat, the widow of Egyptian president Anwar Sadat, and sat across the table from her. At one point the conversation turned to Columbine, with regrets being expressed all around at the devastation and heartache caused by two troubled and misguided youth. One man at the table opined that the failure was rooted in the various law-enforcement agencies who had failed to contain the situation. Mrs. Sadat immediately countered him with words approximate to these: "No, the problem is with our homes. Too many mothers don't know what is happening with their children. Too many mothers have abdicated responsibility for teaching their children what is right. It all begins with mothers." From where I sat, I could see the energy and conviction with which she expressed this truth. She then went on to express her concerns about her own family, and particularly her grandchildren, focusing on the responsibilities she felt as a grandmother to teach and model values.

What values, then, should we as mothers and other female members of the family try to model and teach (by word and deed) to those within our sphere of influence?

We should teach the value of honesty. Dishonesty corrodes the spirit.

When we breach our integrity, not only do others wonder if they can trust us, but we wonder if we can trust ourselves. I have never met a man or woman whose life was better, or who had more peace of mind or self-confidence or feeling of self-worth, because of their dishonesty. In a letter to her friend Abigail Adams, Mercy Otis Warren said that the first thing she should instill in her children was "a sacred regard to Veracity," because it makes everything else come easier (Bennett, *Spirit of America*, 233).

We should teach the virtue of personal moral virtue. Even a casual glance through almost any magazine or newspaper, or at almost any DVD or web site, reveals that many today see morality as old-fashioned, out of date, and unenlightened, and immorality as the hallmark of modern society. And yet, find me the man or woman who is happier and feels better about his or her life because of adultery, or any kind of immorality, for that matter. Immorality breeds not only disease but discontent, lack of self-respect, anxiety, and insecurity.

Our youth don't get that picture at school or online or in the movies or the music world's offerings or from their peers. If they take their cues solely from the world, they'll grow up believing that sexual experience is more important than just about anything else, and that almost anything goes when it comes to sex. The only chance our youth have of learning the virtue of virtue—that it leads to peace of mind, progression, and ultimate happiness—is from us, as we live moral lives and show them the virtue of having virtue and the joy we have in living chaste lives.

Not long ago I joined many others in helping host VIP tours through the Manhattan Temple prior to its dedication. In New York City, this included many from the media world. After going on the tour, one of the media's most venerable and respected reporters asked his tour guides why LDS women were so beautiful. One of the guides responded immediately, "It is because they have the Holy Ghost with them." Another guide added, "And it is because our women are chaste, which is increasingly difficult to find today. Perhaps that is the distinction you are noting."

Indeed, chastity and virtue are beautiful. What a different message from those that our children and youth see depicted and hear from the world! Therefore, it is essential that they hear it from us.

We should teach those we love to stand up for what they believe. Joan of Arc lived what she believed. In the Maxwell Anderson play about the celebrated French peasant girl, Joan says: "Every woman gives her life for what she believes. Sometimes people believe in little or nothing, nevertheless they give up their lives to that little or nothing. One life is all we have, and we live it as we believe in living it, and then it's gone" (*Joan of Lorraine*, act 2).

I was so proud of a niece of mine who went to a sleepover only to find that her friends were excited about watching a movie she knew her parents wouldn't approve of. It was awkward and hard and a little embarrassing, but after trying to encourage her friends to choose another movie, to no avail, she finally slipped into another room to call her mother to come and get her. When the other girls found out she was going home, they immediately switched their choice, and they all enjoyed something different. It took just one young girl to quietly but firmly stick to her beliefs, and all benefited.

We should help our family members learn to serve and care about others more than themselves. The women of the Church are magnificent examples of service. I'll never forget calling my nephew Tanner to congratulate him on completing the major service project he'd undertaken to achieve his Eagle Scout award. His first comment was, "Mom is the one you should tell 'Way to go!' I would have never gotten it done without her!"

And there are countless other virtues we as women are in ideal positions to model. The virtue of work—that almost anything of value requires effort and plain old hard work. The virtue of having tolerance for others who are different, but doing so without surrendering our own values. The virtue of being willing to forgive—and the truth that we can solve almost any problem if we are willing to both apologize and accept an apology. The virtues of kindness and civility, which are marks of spiritually and emotionally mature people. The virtue of understanding the difference between right and wrong. We can make it fashionable again to be good and to do good.

In short, teaching values most effectively begins with us, the women of the family. We teach values every day by the way we live, by what we model for our children and grandchildren, siblings and nieces and nephews. The questions we may wish to ask ourselves, then, might include, Do we tell the truth? Do we bring refinement and strength and optimism to the family? Are we kind? Do we have a graciousness about us? There are few things more unappealing than a coarse, overexposed, immodest, deceitful woman. On the other hand, there are few things more beautiful or delightful than women of integrity and grace and strength who seek to bless those they love.

Another way women have great influence in the family is by nurturing and caring. Nurturing creates a sense of security and stability. It creates a feeling of belonging, and a belonging environment tends to be an environment in which we are most likely to grow, meet challenges head-on, and develop confidence.

A friend who adores his wife said one day when he was a little discouraged that he couldn't wait to get home to just spend some time with her. "Encouragement sounds different to a man when it comes from a woman," he said. "And when it comes from my wife, it affects me more than when it comes from anyone else." His feelings were echoed in what John Adams wrote to his beloved wife Abigail, "I must intreat you, my dear Partner in all the Joys and Sorrows, Prosperity and Adversity of my Life, to take a Part with me in the Struggle" (Bennett, *Spirit of America*, 290).

I can't help but think of a woman I know who with her husband has endured a great deal of struggle and opposition in their marriage. They are still together, but there has been serious tension in their home for years. And yet, their children appear to be doing better than you'd expect. Perhaps the reason is that they have such a splendid mother who has created a safe place for her children despite the uncertainty in her personal life.

Research has shown that women are the buffer in the family. They tend to buffer other family members from uncertainty and worry in times of illness, in times of family stress and crisis, in times of heartache. Women are able to provide such a buffer because their nature is to nurture. They have a tendency to care more about others than themselves.

Another dear friend, a respected leader in many circles, was raised by a widowed mother. They were poor, and his mother struggled to put food on the table. He loved her dearly, but he admits that he was a little embarrassed from time to time because she had only two dresses—one for the weekdays, and one for Sunday—and whenever she needed to come down to the school during the week she wore the same old, faded, though clean and neatly pressed, dress. When he ran for student-body president in high school and won, he wanted his mother at the assembly where his nomination would be announced, but he also worried that she would come wearing her drab, weekday dress. At the assembly he kept scanning the crowd, but he couldn't find her. As he was speaking, accepting the nomination of his peers as their student-body president, out of the corner of his eye he saw her, standing behind the bleachers where she couldn't be seen by others, and yes, wearing her weekday dress.

My friend, now a mature, accomplished man, says, "I will never forget that moment. And I will never forget the lesson I learned in that moment. Mother had somehow sensed that I would be uncomfortable if she were there, and yet she couldn't stay away. But that day I realized that in my mother I had a true champion, someone who would never let me down, someone who cared more about how I would feel than how she felt. Having her there was more important than the entire cheering student body." His mother's caring influence has sustained this man and given him confidence and security throughout his entire life.

When we nurture, we create a sense of belonging and security, we build confidence, and we speed healing—be it emotional or physical.

Another way we as women have profound influence in the family is by building faith. Indeed, we have a natural talent for having faith and building faith. Women are, in many ways, central to the spiritual stability and strength of the family.

Life is tricky. It is filled with glorious moments as well as times of purging, penetrating disappointment. There are days designed to nearly crush us unless we have the assurance that we are not alone in this life. We need to know not only that God is aware of us but that He will help us—if we believe in and seek after Him. We can each expect to have challenges, difficult decisions, and moments of sheer terror. It is our faith in God the Father and His Son Jesus Christ that will fill us with peace and hope, even amidst uncertainty. Faith precedes hope, and optimism is the outgrowth of hope.

I think of a Palestinian woman I was privileged to meet in Jerusalem. She is now in her eighties, widowed, and suffering from cancer. She has lived a full and wonderful life. But it has also been a heartbreaking life. She has fled her home many times and endured countless hardships. She has stared death in the face again and again. When a mutual friend asked this beautiful woman whose face and eyes were filled with light how she had managed to endure so many tragedies, she responded simply, "It is God. God has helped me through."

It is God who helps us do what we have come here to do. The sooner we really come to believe that, the more productive and hopeful and contributing our lives will be. Faith is the core essence of great women.

A Presbyterian friend who loves the Lord and has devoted her life to Him is an example of this. She and her husband were thrilled when she was able to conceive their first child, but then subsequently heartsick when they learned that the fetus had serious chromosomal damage. Specialists in several major children's hospitals encouraged her—nearly commanded her—to abort the baby. She was told that the baby wouldn't survive the birth process, but that if he did he would live but a few hours at most. Nonetheless, she and her husband didn't even consider an abortion. She later explained, "We really never discussed it. We had conceived a baby, and we were going to have the baby. We believed it was all in God's hands." What they did do, though, was begin to pray and to ask their family and friends to pray for them and their baby.

Midway through her pregnancy, she received a call from her mother, who had awakened with a passage from Psalms in her mind: "He trusted on the Lord that he would deliver him: let him deliver him, seeing he delighted in him. But thou art he that took me out of the womb: thou didst make me hope when I was upon my mother's breasts. I was cast upon thee from the womb" (Psalm 22:8–10). Her mother's faith strengthened her faith and gave her the courage to go on.

The long story made short is that my friend's son is now five years old. He has physical challenges, and probably always will, but as she explains it, "He thinks he is the luckiest little boy in the world." That is because he was born into a home and extended family where faith in God governs all that takes place.

The impact of righteous women, and particularly righteous mothers, on their posterity and family members cannot be overstated. Again and again the faith and prayers of Lucy Mack Smith strengthened her family. In one instance, when both Hyrum and Joseph were stricken with what appeared to be a debilitating and perhaps even lethal attack of cholera while in western Missouri separated from their families, they began to pray and determined to stay on their knees until the Lord relieved their suffering. After an extended period of time, at which point it felt as though the disease was beginning to loosen its hold, Hyrum leaped to his feet and exclaimed, "Joseph, we shall return [home], for I have seen an open vision in which I saw Mother on her knees under an apple tree praying for us, and she is even now asking God, in tears, to spare our lives, that she may behold us again in the flesh. The Spirit testifies to me that her prayers and ours shall be heard." From that moment they were healed and went on their way rejoicing (*History of Joseph Smith by His Mother*, 318–19).

Several summers ago my sister lost two children—her fifteen-year-old son named Tanner and her nine-year-old daughter named Amanda—in a horrific automobile accident on a Sunday evening. There are no words to describe the emotional pain associated with such a devastating loss. But there have been tender realizations and moments as well, including reading her son's journal. Just a few days before the accident, Tanner had written, "Thanks mom and dad for teaching me about God." Could my sister and her husband have given their son anything more precious prior to his death than a deep faith in the Lord?

My mother and both of my grandmothers also each lost her eldest son at an early age. Without exception, it has been the faith of these women that has sustained them and their families during difficult, disappointing, heartbreaking times.

I believe there is nothing we as women can do that will have greater significance than to teach and exemplify for those we love that we are not alone in this life, that God will help us, that He cares for us, and that with His help our potential is limitless. There is no more treasured or priceless gift we can give those who look to us as examples than to let them see and experience our faith and our faithfulness.

Nowhere can that take place any better than in the family. The family should be a place of security and safety, a place where we may safely retreat, a place where love and acceptance are the undergirding and prevailing sentiments, where we hear many more positive messages than negative ones. The family should be the place where we can safely be vulnerable, where we develop our resilience, where we replenish our emotional supply, and where we are reminded on a regular, everyday basis about what is important, what is good, and where happiness really comes from.

Women can have unique and penetrating influence in helping those they love learn such time-honored virtues as integrity and morality, kindness and civility—the values that build strong, principled, happy people and strong, principled happy families, and thus inevitably a stronger and more principled world. This happens in particular as we nurture others, care for others, and show what it looks like to care more about others than ourselves. And as we deepen our own faith in God, we can help those we love to do likewise.

Once again, from President Kimball: "The time will come when only those who believe deeply and actively in the family will be able to preserve their families in the midst of the gathering evil around us." It does appear that that time has come. Our Father and His Son are depending on the women of the Church to believe deeply, even passionately, enough about this crucial issue to stand up for what we believe—and particularly to stand in defense of the family as the most vital, vibrant, and unique unit in all of society.

CHAPTER TWELVE

The Trail We're Leaving Behind

❖

We are reaping benefits of the seeds of peace and freedom sown by
our Founding Fathers and others who forged a stunning trail of integrity,
selflessness, and devotion to God. What trail are we leaving
behind us? And what seeds are we sowing?

I CAN STILL REMEMBER WHERE I WAS when it *really* hit me how grateful I was to be an American. I was 40,000 feet above the Pacific Ocean, somewhere between southeast Asia and the west coast of the United States. This wasn't my first trip abroad. Far from it. I'd had many international experiences and had always returned with a greater appreciation for home. But this time, I felt something different, something even more than before. Somehow, the sequence of experiences I'd had on this trip had affected me deeply. Maybe it was seeing so much poverty. Maybe it was meeting so many children orphaned by war. Maybe it was all the people I'd seen who seemed to have no hope. Maybe it was all of the above.

During the long flight, with lots of time to think, I found myself vacillating between gratitude and guilt—gratitude for all I had and guilt because of all I had—until I had a strong and clear impression: I didn't need to feel guilty because of what I had. But because I had more— more opportunities, more privileges, more freedom—I was expected to *do* more. The phrase, "Of him unto whom much is given, much is required" (D&C 82:3) lit up in my mind like a neon sign.

We who are citizens of the United States have, very simply, been given more.

Now, please don't misunderstand. I am not suggesting some kind of arrogant cultural superiority. I deeply love and respect the peoples and cultures of the world. I have seen many of the world's beauties. In nation after nation, I've marveled at magnificent cultures and languages, majestic reminders of antiquity, and people everywhere who are gracious and inspiring and ingenious. Long ago my mother stopped asking me about my trips whenever I return from abroad. Instead she now tells *me* how it went: "I already know what you're going to say. You *loved* the people! You loved their culture. You saw things you'd never seen, thought things you'd never thought. You can't believe how marvelous the experience was. You can't wait to go back." And it's true. That *is* what I always say, because I never lose my sense of awe at the basic wonder of people. I have seen that even in some of the world's most desperate situations, there is always something to marvel about. I have seen for myself that there is beauty and ingenuity almost everywhere.

But that fact notwithstanding, there is simply no country that compares with the United States. There are reasons for this. America is a land of promise, a land choice above all others, founded by noble men inspired by God. Further, America was not only founded by God but has been preserved by Him. Thus, we owe our privileges and prosperity, unequaled anywhere in the world, to Him. But with those privileges come great responsibilities—especially our responsibility to serve God and to live as He would have us live. In short, this land's future is dependent upon the righteousness of its people. That means that we very literally hold the destiny of the United States of America in our hands.

What then are we to do? Perhaps I can illustrate with something my nephew Trevor said when he was about nine. As background, it is important to understand that for years my seventeen nieces and nephews have routinely and regularly prayed that their Aunt Sheri would get married. One morning I answered the phone to hear my brother, Trevor's father, on the other end, laughing. "You should have been here when Trevor blessed the food this morning," he said. "What did Trev say?" I asked, to which my brother responded: "Please bless Aunt Sheri to find a good husband who doesn't smoke, drink, say bad words, or . . . litter!"

Now, I invite you to consider just how profound Trevor's prayer was. There are philosophical ramifications to litter. What is litter? It's not just garbage, but garbage left rudely behind that someone else has to pick up. When all is said and done, I hope the man I marry *doesn't* litter, because there are all kinds of litter in this world, and I'm not just referring to gum wrappers and crushed soft-drink cans.

For example, one morning not long ago I walked into my office and by 10:00 A.M. had managed to offend just about everyone who came within shouting distance. When I came to my senses and realized the trail of litter I was leaving behind me—a trail of ill will and hurt feelings—I retraced my steps and apologized, that day, at least, picking up my own litter. The bottom line is this: We are *all* leaving a trail behind us. The pertinent question is: What kind of trail is it?

Trevor's prayer always makes me think about my grandparents, Charles and Maude Dew, who homesteaded our family farm in the southwest corner of Kansas nearly a century ago. With their two sons, they somehow survived both the Depression and the Dust Bowl, managing to scratch out a meager living on the Great Plains. My respect for their stamina only increased when I came across a letter President Ezra Taft Benson received in 1959 while serving as Secretary of Agriculture— a letter that referred to, *of all people,* my grandparents! The writer of the letter related this: "During the past week-end, I . . . [visited the Dews'] farm and was thrilled with what I saw. West Kansas is . . . no place for a tenderfoot. It takes people who are strong both physically and spiritually to battle the farming conditions in that area. . . . I am writing this letter because I hope that . . . you will have an opportunity to . . . meet this family. You would recognize them as the kind of family that has built the farming areas of this country and you would be inspired by their strength" (letter from Sam R. Carpenter to Ezra Taft Benson, 1 December 1959).

I mention this letter not to boast about my grandparents but because I believe they reflect the character of millions of everyday Americans who have made this country strong. Grandma and Grandpa didn't die rich or famous. They never made the nightly news or the cover of *Time* magazine. They never had their fifteen minutes of fame, so to speak. But on that inconspicuous little farm on the prairie, they learned what all farmers learn naturally and what we all must learn in some way: that you can reap only what you sow. The Apostle Paul taught that "he which soweth sparingly shall reap also sparingly; and he which soweth bountifully shall reap also bountifully" (2 Corinthians 9:6). Grandma and Grandpa planted seeds—literally and figuratively—that have yielded a bountiful harvest. We who descend from them have been shaped by the seeds of integrity and devotion they sowed. We are the beneficiaries of the trail they left behind them—a trail that, fortunately for us, was virtuous.

The cycle of sowing and reaping has been repeated again and again throughout the history of this nation. As the vanguard companies of Mormon pioneers made their epic trek to the Salt Lake Valley in the uncharted American West, they planted crops that they would never harvest, but that would sustain the wagon trains and handcart companies to follow.

Similarly, our Founding Fathers planted seeds of liberty and freedom that have produced centuries of harvest to be reaped by those of us fortunate enough to inherit the privileges and protections guaranteed by the Constitution. The wealth of the United States does not lie in its stock market or entrepreneurial reservoir. America's wealth lies in its people—in us, and in the seeds we are sowing.

There is much evidence in this country of goodness. In the aftermath of 9/11, citizens from coast to coast rallied to help, comfort, and dig through rubble. We'll never hear the words, "Let's roll!" without thinking of heroes who forced down their hijacked plane in a Pennsylvania field to preserve the lives of others elsewhere. We'll never forget the images of firemen charging *up* the Twin Towers stairways as thousands raced down. To quote Anne Frank, "In spite of everything, I still believe that people are really good at heart" (as quoted in *Newsweek*, 20 December 1999, 62). I also truly believe that most people are really good at heart.

However, there are worrisome signs that our collective moral fabric is unraveling. Here are just a few examples of recent moral belly flops:

The two top editors of a venerable newspaper resigned after a trail of journalistic fraud cast a shadow of mistrust on the paper (*New York Times*, 6 June 2003; *Time*, 19 May 2002). The CEO of a media empire resigned after a federal grand jury indicted her on five criminal counts (*Wall Street Journal*, 5 June 2003), and a year later she had been convicted and sentenced to serve time in prison (*New York Times*, 17 July 2004).

A CFO in a major corporation was indicted on 100 charges of fraud, obstruction of justice, insider trading, and money laundering, and the following year the CEO of the same company was indicted on 11 criminal counts, including bank and securities fraud (*USA Today*, 20 May 2003; *U.S. News and World Report*, 19 July 2004); a governor was threatened with recall on charges of financial mismanagement and was subsequently unseated in a special election. Even a self-appointed moral crusader has broken the public trust.

In another arena, no pun intended, three college coaches were fired for lying about everything from immoral liaisons to recruiting violations. In one conference alone, six of twelve schools were either on probation or under NCAA investigation, mostly for coaching misdeeds (*Time*, 19 May 2003). Another athletic hero was arrested on charges of rape. Record-holders in various fields were charged with steroid use. And a baseball hero was suspended after his corked bat shattered.

Regrettably, this brief listing doesn't expose even the tip of what is no doubt a massive iceberg. What trail are we as a people leaving behind us? What kind of harvest can we possibly expect to reap if we are increasingly sowing seeds of deception and deceit?

This is serious. James Madison, who is regarded as the father of the Constitution, put it this way: "We have staked the whole future of American civilization not upon the power of government—far from it. We have staked the future . . . upon the capacity of each . . . of us to govern ourselves according to the Ten Commandments of God" (Walton, *Biblical Principles of Importance to Godly Christians,* 361). My dear friends, here is the sobering reality: Our Constitution was written for a moral people. It will not survive a people who collectively lose their virtue.

We have our problems and we have them aplenty. Little by little, one misdeed, one deception, one self-centered act, one person at a time, the character of the American people is being reshaped. Thus, if we are to change society, we must change ourselves. For one person *can* make a difference. It was *one* woman, the Jewish Queen Esther, who ignored personal danger, spoke truth, and saved a people. Surely the words Mordecai spoke to her apply to us all: "Who knoweth whether thou art come to the kingdom for such a time as this?" (Esther 4:14).

Each of us has a role to play in preserving this nation. The place to reform our country is not Washington, D.C.—though the capital could stand some reformation. The place to begin is with ourselves. If we want to preserve freedom as we know it, *we* must live righteously, for "righteousness exalteth a nation" (Proverbs 14:34). Or as John Adams said on one occasion, "To be good, and to do good is all we have to do" (McCullough, *John Adams,* 170). This is still true in our day, as President George W. Bush said to a Joint Session of Congress nine days after the Twin Towers disaster: "I ask you to uphold the values of America, and remember why so many have come here. We are in a fight for our principles, and *our* first responsibility is to live by them" (*Our Mission and Our Moment*, 9).

America can be no stronger than the goodness of its people. So I repeat: What kind of trail are we leaving behind us? What seeds are we sowing? May I suggest three seeds we must individually sow if we wish to collectively reap a bountiful national harvest. They are the seeds of integrity, selflessness, and devotion to God.

SEED NUMBER ONE: INTEGRITY

Our Founding Fathers clearly understood the crucial importance of integrity. When they signed the Declaration of Independence, they pledged not only their lives and fortunes but their sacred honor. They didn't just moralize about integrity. They modeled it. Said one historian of George Washington: "He never lied, fudged, or cheated. He shared his army's privations. [He] came to stand for the new nation and its republican virtues, which was why he became our first President by unanimous choice" (Ambrose, *To America*, 10). Washington himself admitted, "I hope I shall always possess firmness and virtue enough to maintain what I consider the most enviable of all titles, the character of an 'Honest Man'" (Bennett, *Spirit of America*, 220).

John Adams felt similarly. He told his grandsons: "Have you considered the meaning of that word 'worthy'? . . . I had rather you should be worthy possessors of one thousand pounds honestly acquired by your own labor . . . than of ten millions by banks and tricks. . . . I had rather you should be worthy makers of brooms and baskets than unworthy presidents of the United States procured by intrigue, factious slander and corruption." On another occasion Adams declared, "I never swerved from any principle . . . to obtain a vote. I never sacrificed a friend or betrayed a trust." And when counseling his daughter about choosing a husband he declared, "Daughter! Get you an honest man for a husband. . . . Regard the honor and moral character of the man more than all other circumstances. Think of no other greatness but that of the soul, no other riches but those of the heart. An honest, sensible, humane man, . . . laboring to do good rather than be rich, to be useful rather than make a show, . . . is really the most respectable man in society." It is no wonder that, upon his inauguration as second president, Adams was called "a man of incorruptible integrity" (McCullough, *John Adams,* 668–69, 595, 289, 470).

Honest Abe's reputation was equally well earned. One story is representative. At twenty-four, Lincoln was named postmaster of New Salem, Illinois, at an annual salary of $55.70. But the New Salem office closed before the year was out. It was several years before an agent arrived from Washington to claim the unearned balance of Lincoln's salary—a whopping $17—and by then, his law practice was floundering and Lincoln was broke. But when asked to produce the unearned back pay, Lincoln opened a trunk and removed a yellowed rag bound with string. Inside was the seventeen dollars. The agent was stunned to find the original money untouched. Lincoln said, simply, "I never use any man's money but my own." Imagine what such behavior would do to Wall Street, not to mention Main Street.

Lincoln's moral courage became legendary. His friend and fellow attorney Joseph Gillespie said that Lincoln "was brave without being rash and never refrained from giving utterance to his views because they were unpopular or likely to bring him into danger." Indeed, Lincoln himself said this in an 1839 address: "The probability that we may fail in the struggle ought not to deter us from the support of a cause we believe to be just; it shall not deter me" (Griessman, *Words Lincoln Lived By*, 19).

Everyone wishes to be dealt with honestly, for it is the only way we can build relationships that in turn build our society. And besides, as Mark Twain put it, "If you tell the truth, you don't have to remember anything" (Panati, *Words to Live By*, 22).

SEED NUMBER TWO: SELFLESSNESS

Selfless service has been core to our nation from the beginning. Recently we have again seen dramatic examples of this, as men and women in uniform have put their lives on the line in Afghanistan and again in Iraq to do for us what many of us have not been in a position to do for ourselves. I'll never forget walking through the American Military Cemetery in Manila, where halfway around the world acre after acre of white crosses and Stars of David mark the graves of tens of thousands of Americans who died defending our freedom. That beautiful cemetery in that hot, muggy, distant land felt like hallowed ground.

When in England prior to the war launched in the spring of 2003 against Saddam Hussein, Secretary of State Colin Powell was reportedly asked by the Archbishop of Canterbury if our plans for Iraq were just empire-building. Secretary Powell responded: "Over the years the United States has sent many of its fine young men and women into great peril to fight for freedom beyond our borders. The only amount of land we have asked for is enough to bury those who did not return."

Our history is filled with sterling examples of selfless service. John Adams hinted at the sacrifice he and other Founding Fathers made in a letter to his posterity: "You will never know how much it cost [our] generation to preserve your freedom. I hope you will make good use of it! If you do not, I shall repent in Heaven that I ever took half the pains to preserve it!" (Panati, *Words to Live By*, 255).

Today our opportunities to serve one another are endless. There are causes every one of us can care about: school violence, the homeless, pornography, gangs, addiction and abuse in all their forms, and the list goes on and on. As President Bush said in his 2003 State of the Union address, "Sometimes it takes just one person in someone's life. I urge *you* to be that person." His words mirror Albert Schweitzer's declaration: "One thing I know: the only ones among you who will be really happy are those who will have sought and found how to serve" (Panati, *Words to Live By*, 132).

We are each in a position to make the lives of others better, often in simple ways. For decades, even through bouts of cancer and chemotherapy, every election day has found my mother on duty at the election board from before dawn to way past dusk—just like thousands of other Americans who facilitate our privilege to vote. When I asked Mom why she has served in this way for so long, she said, "They have needed help, and I have been able to help. It has been one small way I could express gratitude for our country." People's willingness to help is what makes America strong.

May I suggest, however, that the most crucial service any of us ever give is in our homes, for the family is the fundamental unit of our society. If the family fails, our country will fail.

There are philosophies afoot, some subtle, some not, that taken together threaten to completely undo our society because they threaten to destroy the family. As an example of just one such subtle philosophy— a village may enrich the life of a child, but a village can *never* take the place of a mother and father who are faithful to each other and dedicated to raising that child. Marriage between a husband and wife is the best environment in which to raise healthy, happy children who become healthy, happy, contributing adults. Thus, there may not be anything we can do to have a more dramatic effect on the strength of our country than to strengthen our families. And it can happen in simple ways.

My homesteading grandmother, who died when I was eleven, has influenced me my entire life. In Grandma's life history she wrote about the accidental death of her thirty-two-year-old son. "This has been a very hard thing for us to take," she wrote. "It has left a great vacancy that cannot be filled in this life." It was, however, the juxtaposition of that thought with Grandma's next sentence that moved me. "But God has been good to us. And I wish to say for the benefit of our posterity, do not ever be slack in your duties. . . . We must always be found defending truth. And we must be found teaching it by our every word and action."

I came across these pages recently during a week when I'd had one disillusioning episode after another. I was so discouraged. I felt spent—until I read Grandma's words. Her faith strengthened my faith. Her resolve reinforced mine. Her determination to go on despite despair inspired me to go on. Once again, I harvested the fruits of seeds she planted long ago.

The family *should* be where we replenish our emotional supply, for it is the best place to find the courage to be more and do more than we can be or do on our own. Every time a family is strengthened, our nation grows stronger.

SEED NUMBER THREE: DEVOTION TO GOD

I can vividly remember when history came alive for me—when I realized that history was not just obscure facts in dusty old books, but that it was about real people. I was in Istanbul looking at the ancient wall that surrounds that city, a wall that was built during the Ottoman Empire. I found myself wanting to know more about the people who had lived there and then, and what motivated them to build such a wall.

I love trying to understand what motivates people—and particularly those who laid the foundations of this country, for our history is a spiritually stirring saga. There are some today who feel God shouldn't play a role in our public lives, but anyone who knows our history realizes our Founding Fathers didn't see it that way at all. Columbus recorded this: "Our Lord unlocked my mind, sent me upon the sea, and gave me fire for the deed. Those who heard of my enterprise called it foolish, mocked me, and laughed. But who can doubt but that the Holy Ghost inspired me?" (Wasserman, *Columbus, Don Quixote of the Seas,* 19–20).

Most who came to this new world believed it had been reserved by God for His purposes. The Pilgrims of Plymouth, the Calverts of Maryland, Roger Williams, William Penn, and many others had deep religious convictions that drove them to this land. John Winthrop preached that his people had covenanted with God to obtain a new place and government (see McLaughlin, *Foundations of American Constitutionalism,* 33). And when the Pilgrims landed in this hemisphere, Governor William Bradford recorded, "They fell upon their knees and blessed the God of Heaven" (as quoted in Benson, *God, Family, Country,* 115).

Later, on the eve of the Revolution, Patrick Henry declared that "there is a just God who presides over the destinies of nations, and who will raise up friends to fight our battles for us" (as quoted in Benson, *This Nation Shall Endure,* 68–69).

And raise up friends He did, for that ragtag band of Colonists should never have won the Revolutionary War. They were outmanned, outmaneuvered, outsmarted, and outgunned again and again by a superior British army. Yet they prevailed. Surely the only explanation is the intervention of God.

That is certainly to Whom George Washington attributed the victory, stating in his first Inaugural Address: "No People can be bound to acknowledge and adore the invisible hand, which conducts the Affairs of men more than the People of the United States. Every step . . . seems to have been distinguished by some token of providential agency" (Bennett, *Spirit of America*, 381–82).

A few years later, when a deadlock gripped the Constitutional Convention, Benjamin Franklin urged that "henceforth prayers imploring the assistance of Heaven, and its blessings on our deliberation, be held in this Assembly every morning before we proceed to business" (*Notes of the Debates in the Federal Convention of 1787 Reported by James Madison*, xxiii). The Constitution that resulted from that convention was itself revolutionary. Wrote convention delegate Charles Pickney: "When the great work [of the Constitution] was done . . . I was . . . struck with amazement. Nothing less than that superintending hand of Providence, that so miraculously carried us through the war . . . could have brought it about so complete" (Ford, ed., *Essays on the Constitution*, 412).

Indeed, the Constitution—which is the most significant legislative document ever adopted by a people—exceeded the genius of the delegates. Surely it was the work of principled men inspired by God—men who not only believed in God but believed that God was guiding *them*.

This rich heritage of divine guidance makes some developments today hard to understand. I cite as an example the recent court decision

banning the Pledge of Allegiance from schoolrooms because of its reference to God. Of course, this wasn't the first. A few years ago the state
of New Jersey passed a law deleting any mention of God from court-
room oaths. Not long thereafter, another judge banned Bibles for deliv-
ering such oaths because "you-know-who [was] mentioned inside"
(*Wall Street Journal*, 31 July 1996, A13). And in another state such a
ruckus was raised over a display of the Ten Commandments outside the
state's Supreme Court that it was eventually removed—over the loud
protests of that state's chief justice.

Such developments are frightening. Those who insist that God has
no place in our public discourse simply do not understand the fundamental premise upon which this country was founded and *upon which it
depends*. Freedom isn't always lost on the battlefield.

Those who have launched such vigorous objections to anything
mentioning God clearly do not understand that God has been part of
this country from its inception, and evidence of His influence is almost
everywhere you look. The two huge oak doors that give entrance into
the United States Supreme Court have the Ten Commandments
engraved upon them. There are biblical verses etched in stone on federal buildings and monuments throughout Washington, D. C. Every
session of Congress begins with an invocation by a minister whose
salary has been paid by the taxpayer since 1777.

Of course, despite these evidences of the feelings of the Founding
Fathers, an avoidance of God on the part of some is not new. During the
darkest days of the Civil War, President Lincoln called for a national day
of fasting and prayer, declaring: "We have been recipients of the choic-
est bounties of Heaven; . . . we have grown in number, wealth, and
power as no other Nation has ever grown. But we have forgotten God.

We have forgotten the gracious hand which . . . enriched and strengthened us, and we have vainly imagined . . . that all these blessings were produced by some superior wisdom and virtue of our own. Intoxicated with . . . success we have become . . . too proud to pray to the God that made us. It behooves us . . . to humble ourselves before the offended power." Lincoln concluded by stating, simply: "Those nations only are blessed whose God is the Lord" (Hill, *Abraham Lincoln: Man of God,* 391).

I wonder what Abraham Lincoln would think of us today. Have we too become intoxicated with our wealth and world domination? Have we become so arrogant that we actually believe *we* are the ones who have engineered our prosperity? Have we been given so much for so long that we take our privileges for granted? Have we become so self-important and sophisticated that we have forgotten God? What unspeakable arrogance, to believe that we are somehow responsible for our blessings!

Such trends and attitudes, if they persist unchecked, do not bode well, for as Washington said: "The . . . smiles of Heaven can never be expected on a nation that disregards the eternal rules of order and right, which Heaven itself has ordained" ("Washington's First Inaugural Address," in *Harvard Classics,* 43:243).

More recently, President Gordon B. Hinckley said this: "We are forgetting God, whose commandments we have put aside and obey not. In all too many ways we have substituted human sophistry for the wisdom of the Almighty. . . . Can we expect peace and prosperity . . . while turning our backs on the source of our strength?" ("America Must Look to God," 33–34).

The answer is no. President Lincoln declared, "I have felt [God's] hand upon me in great trials and submitted to His guidance, and I trust that as He shall further open the way I will be ready to walk therein, relying on His help and trusting in His . . . wisdom" (Sandburg, *Abraham Lincoln: The Prairie Years and The War Years*). More recently, some have criticized President George W. Bush for openly acknowledging his dependence upon God. But I find comfort in knowing that the man who can send us to war is humble enough to pray about it. Those who look to God, believe in Him, and serve Him are simply doing what our Founding Fathers did—and making our country stronger in the process. Is it time for all of us to once again humble ourselves before God? For make no mistake about it: We *are* one nation under God.

A couple of years ago I had the poignant experience of visiting the Hiroshima Peace Park. I was accompanied on the visit by the local mission president and two sister missionaries who helped serve as interpreters. As emotionally moving as the memorial was, what touched me most was the fact that Sister Nawahine from Pearl Harbor, Hawaii, and Sister Kato from Tokyo, Japan—whose countries' bitter war led to the devastation at Hiroshima—toured the park arm in arm, the best of friends. Their friendship stood in stark contrast to the hatred of their forebears. That day, I saw firsthand that devotion to God *can* heal all wounds, bridge all cultures, and bless us with peace and freedom.

We are reaping benefits of the seeds of peace and freedom sown by our Founding Fathers and others who forged a stunning trail of integrity, selflessness, and devotion to God. What trail are we leaving behind *us*? And what seeds are *we* sowing?

None of us live only for ourselves. Everything we do affects others. Our collective breaches of integrity and misdeeds could eventually bring our nation down. Our collective virtue can make America stronger than it has ever been.

I like what Abigail Adams wrote to her husband, John, during a troubling time: "You cannot be . . . an inactive spectator. We have too many high sounding words, and too few actions that correspond with them" (McCullough, *John Adams*, 21).

Those of us who know we are living in a land created by God for the benefit of a moral people cannot afford to be inactive spectators if we wish to preserve the destiny of this nation. We repay the goodness in our own lives by investing in the lives of others. Every man and woman, boy and girl, can make a difference. Every young adult, every family, every homemaker and CEO and professor, those who are wealthy and those who are not, black and white and brown, old and young and in-between, those who were born here and those who have been adopted into the American family—*every one* of us can make a difference by the seeds we sow and the trail we leave behind us. Those who live with integrity, who give of themselves, and who never forget that God is the Presiding Authority in the universe are destined to do good and be good. And *that* is what will continue to make America great.

I am not suggesting that any of us attempt to achieve some unrealistic form of perfection, but I do believe it is possible to be perfectly honest every day. I believe it is possible to live so that others can trust our motives, our judgment, and our word. I believe it is possible to forget ourselves and make life better for someone else through some kind of ongoing selfless service—especially service in our families. And I believe it is not only possible but vital that we strengthen our devotion to God by doing a better job of living as His children ought to live.

There is a statement inscribed on a wall in the Library of Congress:

"The history of the world is the biography of great men." I would add "and great women" to that thought. Note that it doesn't say famous men or women, wealthy men or women, gorgeous men or women, or skinny men or women. It says *great* men and women—which I take to mean good men and women.

I will never forget the first time I saw the Lincoln Memorial. It was after dark, and as I climbed the stairs leading up to the monument, what I saw caught my breath: a majestic statue of our sixteenth president, seated as though presiding over the whole of Washington, D.C. I had read enough about Lincoln to know that nothing in his life had come easy. I knew he had felt alone and stood alone again and again. That is probably why my eyes filled with tears as I read the inscription engraved above his head: "In this temple, as in the hearts of the people for whom he saved the union, the memory of Abraham Lincoln is enshrined forever."

It is not surprising that it was Lincoln who, in the midst of the Civil War, described the situation in which we once again find ourselves: "We cannot escape history. We . . . will be remembered in spite of ourselves. . . . We know how to save the Union. The world knows we . . . know how to save it. . . . We shall nobly save, or meanly lose, the last, best, hope of earth" (McDonald, *Lincoln*, 398).

You and I cannot escape history either. We will be remembered in spite of ourselves. We do know how to preserve this union. We can do our part by living with integrity, serving others, and devoting ourselves to God.

In those moments when you consider what it means to be a citizen of this great nation, I hope you'll think about the wise words of a terrific nine-year-old as he prayed for his aunt. I hope you'll think long and hard about the trail you're leaving behind, the seeds you are sowing, and the seeds you wish to sow. And I hope you might join with me in accepting the invitation to identify ways you can live with greater integrity, more selflessness, and greater devotion to God.

May we each go forward, determined to keep America great by keeping America good. God will help us. We are His children. This is His nation. And if we will turn to Him, He Himself will help us preserve this great land of liberty.

CHAPTER THIRTEEN

No One Can Take
Your Place

No one can have the influence you have been prepared
to have on all who come within your sphere of influence.
Without question, no one can fulfill your foreordained mission.
No one can do what you were sent here to do. No one.

I CAN STILL VIVIDLY REMEMBER the April 1973 general conference. I was one of what must have been hundreds of BYU students who had arrived at Temple Square in the wee hours of the morning with the hope of getting a seat in the Tabernacle. But that is not the reason I can remember a conference that was held more than thirty years ago. It is because of what happened when we got inside and the conference began. That morning, when Elder Marvin J. Ashton of the Quorum of the Twelve rose to speak, he began by telling the story of a young man who in Elder Ashton's presence had referred to himself as a "nobody." Elder Ashton's response to that man was that nobody is a nobody.

When Elder Ashton spoke those words, my heart began to pound, and tears began to pool in my eyes. I was all ears as Elder Ashton went on to say: "I am certain our Heavenly Father is displeased when we refer to ourselves as 'nobody.' . . . We do ourselves a great injustice when we allow ourselves, through tragedy, misfortune, challenge, discouragement, or whatever the earthly situation, to so identify ourselves. No matter how or where we find ourselves, we cannot with any justification label ourselves 'nobody.' As children of God we are somebody" (in *Conference Report,* April 1973, 20–21).

At that point in my life, I wasn't so sure. I felt like a nobody. All the evidence seemed to point in that direction. The details aren't important, but I can sum them up by saying I didn't have even a modicum of self-confidence or self-worth. For too many years I had felt that I wasn't talented enough, thin enough, smart enough, cute enough, or basically anything enough to amount to much. There are a hundred and one incidents that would illustrate this. Suffice it to say that when I stepped foot on the BYU campus as a young freshman in the fall of 1971, I must have been the most shy, least accomplished coed on campus. My clothes weren't right. I was desperately homesick. My lack of social skills, combined with my shyness, was deadly on a college campus. Although my goal had always been to get a university degree, I didn't have any idea what I wanted to be or do. I was one pathetic excuse for a university student, or at least, I felt that way. Perhaps just one story will sufficiently illustrate the condition of my life and my frame of mind at that point.

I had grown up playing basketball in the great basketball state of Kansas, and had had some success on the court. More than anything, I wanted to play ball for BYU. So, my shyness notwithstanding, I found out where and when team tryouts were being held and showed up at a certain gym in the Richards P. E. Building at the appointed hour. But when I pulled open the gym door and peeked inside, a group of girls were already running drills. And they looked good! Clearly, I wasn't in Kansas anymore. Suddenly, every insecure cell in my body began to scream, "*What are you thinking?* You aren't good enough to play ball here! You can't compete with these girls! What has gotten into your head!" I quickly closed the door and told myself that if I just had a few minutes to regain some composure, I would go in. I began to pace up and down the hallway outside that gym, telling myself that at any moment I would go in. I paced and paced . . . for three hours I paced— until the tryouts were over. I am sorry to say that I never went in.

It was dark as I walked back to my dorm. I was completely disgusted with myself. I couldn't believe I hadn't at least had the courage to try! I could not believe that I had let my fear dash a childhood dream. And as silly as it may seem, my failure to try out has nagged at me like a sliver ever since. For thirty years now, I haven't been able to watch a women's collegiate basketball game without kind of wincing, all the while wondering if I could have made that team.

Now fast forward thirty years from the fall of 1971 to the fall of 2001, when I was invited to speak to the female athletes at BYU who had made the various intercollegiate teams—the swimmers and divers, the cross-country team, the volleyball and softball teams, the golfers, the soccer team, and of course the basketball team. I was thrilled. I *love* young adults, and to be with young adults who were athletes promised to be a real treat.

That night, as part of my remarks, I told for the first time the story of pacing outside that gymnasium in the fall of 1971. I wanted those young athletes to believe it when I told them how much I admired and respected what they had already accomplished in their lives. When I had concluded, BYU's storied women's athletic director, Dr. Elaine

Michaelis, went to the podium and in front of the audience asked, "Sheri, is that story about you being too shy to try out for the 1971 basketball team really true?" "Yes," I responded.

"Did you know that *I* was the coach of the 1971 BYU women's basketball team?" she continued. "Yes," I answered, adding that through all of these years her name had been emblazoned in my mind, and I had followed with great interest the very successful basketball and volleyball teams she had coached.

"Would you like to know something interesting about my 1971 basketball team?" she went on. I nodded that I would. "In all my years of coaching, it is the *only* year I was not able to fill my roster, and we played that season one player short. All season I kept searching for one more girl to fill out our team, but I could never find her."

Ugh! When she said those words, it felt as though she had suckerpunched me. I couldn't believe it was true, but Elaine later assured me that it was. She had looked all season long for another player to add to her roster, but she had never been able to find that one particular ballplayer.

All the way home I stewed about what she had said. And frankly, I've thought and pondered the matter a great deal since then. Though I suppose I won't know this definitively until I step across the veil and understand many things more clearly, I have a suspicion about all of this. I have the feeling that that spot on that team was mine. But because I didn't even have the courage to step forward and try, it didn't get filled.

For the sake of discussion, let's just assume that that spot could have been mine. Think of the experiences I missed out on by not participating on the team that year. And if I was half as good as I remember myself being, perhaps I could have helped the team. Maybe I could have made a difference. But we'll never know, because I didn't have the self-confidence to even try.

Here's the principle that my sorry brush with the 1971 BYU's women's basketball team has taught me: *No one can take your place.*

Oh, sure, we have all let others down and watched someone else step in to fill the gap, and we've all at times helped fill the gap when others have let us down. So, yes, it's possible to fill in for someone. But it's not possible to take their place. Not now, not ever.

No one can take *your* place in your family or with your friends. No one can take your place in your ward or your extended family, in your neighborhood or at the company where you work. No one can have the influence you have been prepared to have on all who come within your sphere of influence. Without question, no one can fulfill *your* foreordained mission. No one can do what you were sent here to do. No one.

This principle is particularly easy to grasp and understand when someone is gone. It has now been four years since our family lost the two children I mentioned earlier. I never cease to marvel that though both of them lived a relatively few years, no one can fill the gap they have left. We're muddling along without them, but the space they filled hasn't been and can never be filled by anyone else. We never have a family gathering where someone isn't constantly referring to both of them. "Remember when Tanner said . . ." "Remember the way Amanda used to . . ." And on and on. As we continue to miss them in deep and penetrating ways, there is something sweet about the reassurance that nothing and no one can make us forget them or forget the effect they have had on all of us, both in life and in death.

A few days after the passing of Elder Neal A. Maxwell, I pulled off of my "Elder Maxwell Shelf"—and it is an entire shelf—a copy of one of his first books, *A More Excellent Way,* which I purchased in 1973 as a young BYU student. It is dog-eared, full of notes in the margins, and has more paragraphs underlined than not. Opening the book unleashed a flood of memories and emotions about the impact the words of this inspiring leader had on me not only at a pivotal time in my life but ever since. It simply would not be possible to measure the influence his teachings have had on me.

It's difficult to imagine a general conference without Elder Maxwell. I have studied, pondered, and hung on his every word for decades now. He had such a distinctive and spiritually stimulating way of teaching the gospel. No one can take his place, which is a sobering thought.

On the other hand, there is something reassuring about the reality that no one else can step in and do it quite as he did. Others will be called, those who have been refined and prepared by the Lord, and they too will make their own contributions, which also won't be duplicated by others. I look forward to them. But through it all, no one leader can take the place of another. Each is needed. Each is unique. And I find that reality reassuring.

There are many examples of this principle. Consider, for example, the ministry and service of President Harold B. Lee. Because of his youthfulness when called to the Twelve, for several decades Church members had anticipated the day when he would become President of the Church—which he did on July 7, 1972. But then, on December 26, 1973, something unimaginable happened. The comparatively young President Lee, who had been expected to provide many years of vigorous leadership, died suddenly. He was just seventy-four years old, and there had been no warning. It is not an overstatement to say that the entire Church was stunned.

President Spencer W. Kimball, whose health had been tenuous for years, was ordained President of the Church. Later, in a general conference address, Elder William Grant Bangerter of the Seventy gave voice to the feelings many members had no doubt experienced. Said Elder Bangerter: "Suddenly [President Lee] was gone!—called elsewhere after only 1 1/2 years. It was the first time since the death of the Prophet Joseph Smith when the president had died before it was time for him to die. In deep sorrow and concern the surging questions arose in the minds of the people. . . . 'What will we do now? How can we carry on without the prophet? . . . Can the Church survive this emergency?'

"Of course we knew that the Church would survive, but it could not possibly be the same. We had never expected Spencer W. Kimball to become the president, and we had not looked to him for the same leadership evident in the life of Harold B. Lee. We knew, of course, that he would manage somehow, until the next great leader arose, but it would not be easy for him, and things would not be the same. 'Oh, Lord,' we prayed, 'please bless President Kimball. He needs all the help you can give him.' Such seemed to be the attitude in the hearts of the Latter-day Saints during those days of mourning."

Elder Bangerter then went on to describe something that happened during the first general conference following President Lee's death. The General Authorities had gathered to receive counsel and instruction from the First Presidency and the Twelve. Elder Bangerter recounted: "The moment came when President Kimball arose to address the assembled leadership. He noted that he also had never expected to occupy this position and that he missed President Lee equally with the rest of us. . . . As he proceeded with his address, however, he had not spoken very long when a new awareness seemed suddenly to fall on the congregation. We became alert to an astonishing spiritual presence, and we realized that we were listening to something unusual, powerful, different from any of our previous meetings. It was as if, spiritually speaking, our hair began to stand on end. . . . President Kimball spoke under this special influence for an hour and ten minutes. It was a message totally unlike any other in my experience. . . . When President Kimball concluded, President Ezra Taft Benson arose and with a voice filled with emotion, echoing the feeling of all present, said, in substance: 'President Kimball, through all the years that these meetings have been held, we have never heard such an address as you have just given. Truly, there is a prophet in Israel'" ("A Special Moment in Church History," 26–27).

President Kimball could not take President Harold B. Lee's place, nor did he try to. He had his own place, his own assignments, his own contribution to make, just as President Lee did so magnificently during his time on earth.

Like the little girl on the cover of this book, hard at work tending her own little plot of ground, we each came here with our own plot of ground, as it were, our own little corner of the Lord's vineyard to tend and build. No one can do it for us. We can help each other—in fact, it is incumbent upon each of us to help and assist and strengthen one another. As Alma taught, those who have taken upon themselves the name of Christ and entered into the waters of baptism covenant to impart unto one another "temporally and spiritually according to their needs and their wants" (Mosiah 18:29). But nonetheless, we each must put one foot in front of the other, and work day in and day out to do what we came here to do and to fulfill the assignments that are ours and ours alone.

I thought about this again on a recent trip to Nauvoo. I have written before about the fact that Nauvoo always moves me. I find myself contemplating and considering things there that never seem to occur to me elsewhere. I'll never forget the first time I stood at the end of Parley Street and tried to imagine how it would have felt to pack up a few belongings, close the door, walk away from home (for perhaps the third or fourth time), and join the growing line of wagons waiting to ferry across the Mississippi, knowing I would probably never be back. President Hugh B. Brown stated that "history rests on the shoulders of those who accepted the challenges of difficulties and drove through to victory in spite of everything" (*Abundant Life,* 139). It's difficult to imagine any group of men and women to whom this applies more than to those who laid the foundation of the gospel kingdom in this dispensation.

While in Nauvoo this latest time, I did what I always do: I walked to the end of Parley Street early in the morning when the dew was still on the grass and only the birds were awake. At that time of day, when the air is clear and crisp and the morning smells fresh, it's as though you can hear the sounds and smell the smells that Joseph and Brigham, Parley and Heber, Eliza and Mary Fielding and Bathsheba would have heard and smelled. It's easier to imagine what our friends must have experienced in their day.

I call them our friends because I believe we were and are probably the dearest of friends. Elder Bruce R. McConkie taught that "we went to school in preexistence. There were occasions when Adam taught the classes, and when Abraham taught the classes, and when Joseph Smith did. And the classes were so numerous and so extensive that the whole house of Israel—that group of spirits who were foreordained to become Israelites—were teachers; and they taught classes. And the witness of truth was borne and we were given the opportunity to advance and progress. When the time came for us to come down to mortality, we ended a course of instruction that had been going on for an infinitely long period of time. . . . In effect, this mortal course is the final examination for all of the life that we lived through in this infinite premortal period" (*Doctrines of the Restoration,* 340–41).

Does it not seem possible, perhaps even likely, that those of us who were to live in the Dispensation of the Fulness of Times spent time in class together and became acquainted in *other* ways? Surely we were prepared for the unique circumstances we would face during our difficult days on earth. Surely, from the other side of the veil, we cheered for the pioneers, prayed for them, and were pulling for our friends as they put one foot in front of the other in an effort to do what only they could do. Surely we handed out something like high-fives all around as we saw one after another of our fellow Saints stand firm in the fire. Surely we shouted for joy when, in spite of it all, they did not flinch.

Now the tables have turned. They have finished their mortal probation. They did what only they could do in laying the foundation of the Restoration. Now they are on the other side of the veil, and we are here, with our own assignments to build upon what they began and to carry on. Does it not seem possible, perhaps even likely, that they are cheering us on and praying and pulling for us, and helping us in every way they are allowed? As much as we revere the remarkable legacy they established in laying the foundations of this dispensation—for we stand on the shoulders of all who have gone before us—they most likely have similar respect for us. Though no one could take their place, neither can they take ours.

We are not, most of us, forced to leave our homes, bear and bury children along the trail, and push handcarts over Rocky Ridge. Nonetheless, life in the twenty-first century is plenty rocky in its own right. Elder Neal A. Maxwell said it this way: "Though we have rightly applauded our ancestors for their spiritual achievements . . . those of us who prevail today will have done no small thing. The special spirits who have been reserved to live in this time of challenges and who overcome will one day be praised for their stamina by those who pulled handcarts" (*Notwithstanding My Weakness*, 18).

This is the eleventh hour—the last time that the Lord is calling laborers into His vineyard. And even though His vineyard has become corrupted every whit, and there are but few (relatively) who do good, nonetheless He has promised to gather His elect from the four quarters of the earth (see D&C 33:3–7).

Here is the simple, stunning, sobering truth: It takes the elect to gather the elect. That is who we are. And no one can take our place in doing it—whether it be our place in our families, or among our colleagues and friends, or in our wards and neighborhoods, or in the PTAs or board rooms of America, or in the world at large. No one, absolutely no one, can do what we have been sent here to do.

Neither the timing nor the placement of our advent into mortality is accidental or capricious. We are where we are supposed to be. The Lord has put the future of the family, the future of the Church, indeed the future of all society in our hands. If that seems a bit too much to comprehend or to tackle, never forget that it is with us as it was with

Helaman when he said to his band of 2,000 young sons: "Our God is with us, and he will not suffer that we should fall" (Alma 56:46).

God *is* with us. He placed us here now, in whatever circumstances we enjoy and encounter, because He had confidence that we would stand firm in the fire and would not flinch at either the spiritual or the temporal onslaughts of the last days. That will happen as we seek after the Father and the Son, for, as President Ezra Taft Benson taught, "men and women who turn their lives over to God will discover that He can make a lot more out of their lives than they can. He will deepen their joys, expand their vision, quicken their minds, . . . lift their spirits, multiply their blessings, increase their opportunities, comfort their souls, raise up friends, and pour out peace" ("Jesus Christ—Gifts and Expectations," 4).

Indeed, if we will seek after our Father, and seek to follow His Son, They will help us. They will make us equal to all that lies in our path. Our Father already gave us His Son, who in turn gave us His life. From the Father and the Son derive all of the power and strength to do exactly what we came here to do. About this President Boyd K. Packer has taught, "When you say, 'I can't! I can't solve my problems!' I want to thunder out, 'Don't you realize who you are? Haven't you learned yet that you are a son or a daughter of Almighty God? Do you not know that there are powerful resources inherited from Him that you can call upon to give you steadiness and courage and great power?'" ("Self-Reliance," 88).

Surely, premortally, as we withstood the most terrifying of battles and in spite of it all stood loyally by God and by Jesus and did not flinch—surely we committed to our Father and His Son, to each other, and to ourselves that we would come here and do it all over again, this time removed from Their presence.

It behooves us, then, to understand that the Lord knows who we are, where we are, what our mission is, and what we need in order to accomplish that mission. Not only has He known us for a long, long time, He has loved us for a long, long time. We are here now because we are supposed to be here now. No one else can have the influence or do the good that we were prepared and foreordained to have and do. No one else can fulfill our individual missions.

In one of Sir Winston Churchill's famous World War II broadcasts, delivered on 9 February 1941, he declared: "We shall not fail or falter; we shall not weaken or tire. Neither the sudden shock of battle, nor the long-drawn trials of vigilance and exertion will wear us down. . . . We will finish the job" (*The Great Republic*, 323).

Neither will we fall, falter, or tire. President Hinckley's optimism and vision will help us, for, as he said: "I see a wonderful future in a very uncertain world. If we will cling to our values, if we will build on our inheritance, if we will walk in obedience before the Lord, if we will simply live the gospel we will be . . . looked upon as a peculiar people who have found the key to a peculiar happiness. . . . Great has been our past, wonderful is our present, glorious can be our future. . . . We have glimpsed the future, we know the way, we have the truth. God help us to move forward to become a great and mighty people spread over the earth" ("Look to the Future," 69).

No one but you can determine if you will be firm in the fire. No one but you can determine if, at all costs, you will in this sphere stand loyally by God and by Jesus and will not flinch.

For no one, in this grand plan of our Father, can take your place.

Sources Cited

Ambrose, Stephen E. *To America*. New York: Simon and Schuster, 2002.

Anderson, Maxwell. *Joan of Lorraine: A Play in Two Acts*. Washington, D.C.: Anderson House, 1947.

Ballard, Melvin J. *Sermons and Missionary Services of Melvin Joseph Ballard*. Bryant S. Hinckley, comp. Salt Lake City: Deseret Book, 1949.

Bangerter, W. Grant. "A Special Moment in Church History." *Ensign*, November 1977, 26–27.

Bennett, William J. *The Spirit of America*. New York: Simon and Schuster, 1997.

Benson, Ezra Taft. "The Book of Mormon—Keystone of Our Religion." *Ensign*, November 1986, 4–7.

———. *God, Family, Country: Our Three Great Loyalties*. Salt Lake City: Deseret Book, 1974.

———. "Jesus Christ—Gifts and Expectations." *Ensign*, December 1988, 2–6.

———. *This Nation Shall Endure*. Salt Lake City: Deseret Book, 1977.

Brown, Hugh B. *The Abundant Life*. Salt Lake City: Bookcraft, 1965.

Bush, George W. *Our Mission and Our Moment: President George W. Bush's Address to the Nation Before a Joint Session of Congress, September 20, 2001*. Washington, D.C.: Newmarket Press, 2001.

Cannadine, David, ed. *Speeches of Winston Churchill*. London: Penguin Books, 1990.

Cannon, George Q. *Gospel Truth: Discourses and Writings of George Q. Cannon*. Jerreld L. Newquist, ed. Salt Lake City: Deseret Book, 1987.

———. "Topics of the Times." *Juvenile Instructor* 22 (1 May 1887):140.

Churchill, Sir Winston. *The Great Republic*. Winston S. Churchill, ed. New York City: The Modern Library, 2001.

Clark, J. Reuben, Jr. "Our Wives and Our Mothers in the Eternal Plan." *Relief Society Magazine*, December 1946, 801.

Clark, James R., comp. *Messages of the First Presidency of The Church of Jesus Christ of Latter-day Saints.* 6 vols. Salt Lake City: Bookcraft, 1965–75.

Conference Reports of The Church of Jesus Christ of Latter-day Saints.

Cowley, Matthew. *Matthew Cowley Speaks.* Salt Lake City: Deseret Book, 1954.

Dew, Sheri. *Ezra Taft Benson: A Biography.* Salt Lake City: Deseret Book, 1987.

———. *Go Forward with Faith: The Biography of Gordon B. Hinckley.* Salt Lake City: Deseret Book, 1996.

Ehat, Andrew F., and Lyndon W. Cook, eds. *The Words of Joseph Smith: The Contemporary Accounts of the Nauvoo Discourses of the Prophet Joseph.* Second edition, revised. Salt Lake City: Bookcraft, 1996.

Emerging Trends, vol. 21, no. 7 (September 1999).

"The Family: A Proclamation to the World." Salt Lake City: The Church of Jesus Christ of Latter-day Saints, 1995.

Faust, James E. "What It Means to Be a Daughter of God." *Ensign*, November 1999, 100–102.

Ford, P. L. *Essays on the Constitution.* 1892.

Griessman, Gene. *Words Lincoln Lived By.* New York: Fireside, 1997.

The Harvard Classics. 50 vols. Charles W. Eliot, ed. New York: P. F. Collier and Son.

Hill, John Wesley. *Abraham Lincoln: Man of God.* New York: G. P. Putnam's Sons, 1927.

Hinckley, Gordon B. "America Must Look to God." In *The Spirit of America: Patriotic Addresses from America's Freedom Festival.* Salt Lake City: Bookcraft, 1998, 29–37.

———. "The Dawning of a Brighter Day." *Ensign*, May 2004, 81–84.

———. "An Ensign to the Nations, a Light to the World." *Ensign*, November 2003, 82–85.

———. "God Shall Give unto You Knowledge by His Holy Spirit." *BYU Speeches of the Year.* Provo, Utah: Brigham Young University Press, 1973.

———. "If Ye Be Willing and Obedient." *Ensign*, July 1995, 2–5.

———. "The Loneliness of Leadership." BYU Devotional, 4 November 1969.

———. "Look to the Future." *Ensign*, November 1997, 67–69.

———. "Stand Up for Truth." *Brigham Young University Speeches 1996–1997.* Provo, Utah: Brigham Young University, 1997, 21–26.

———. *Standing for Something: 10 Neglected Virtues That Will Heal Our Hearts and Homes.* New York: Random House, 2000.

———. *Teachings of Gordon B. Hinckley.* Salt Lake City: Deseret Book, 1997.

———. "Walking in the Light of the Lord." *Ensign*, November 1998, 97–100.

———. "Watch the Switches in Your Life." *Ensign*, January 1973, 91–93.

———. "We Have a Work to Do." *Ensign*, May 1995, 87–88.

Journal of Discourses. 26 vols. London: Latter-day Saints' Book Depot, 1854–1886.

Kimball, Edward L. *Spencer W. Kimball*. Salt Lake City: Bookcraft, 1977.

Kimball, Spencer W. "Privileges and Responsibilities of Sisters." *Ensign*, November 1978, 102–6.

———. "The Role of Righteous Women." *Ensign*, November 1979, 102–4.

———. *The Teachings of Spencer W. Kimball*. Edward L. Kimball, ed. Salt Lake City: Bookcraft, 1982.

"Laura Bush, Comforter in Chief," from WashingtonPost.com, 21 September 2001.

Lee, Harold B. *BYU Speeches of the Year,* 1956, 2.

———. *The Teachings of Harold B. Lee*. Clyde J. Williams, ed. Salt Lake City: Bookcraft, 1996.

Lewis, C. S. *A Mind Awake: An Anthology of C. S. Lewis*. Clyde S. Kilby, ed. New York: Harcourt Brace, 2003.

———. *The Screwtape Letters*. New York: Touchstone, 1996.

Madsen, Truman G. *Defender of the Faith: The B. H. Roberts Story*. Salt Lake City: Bookcraft, 1980.

———. *The Highest in Us*. Salt Lake City: Bookcraft, 1978.

Maxwell, Neal A. "Encircled in the Arms of His Love." *Ensign*, November 2002, 16–18.

———. *Notwithstanding My Weakness*. Salt Lake City: Deseret Book, 1981.

McConkie, Bruce R. "Be Valiant in the Fight of Faith." *Ensign*, November 1974, 33–35.

———. *Doctrinal New Testament Commentary*. 3 vols. Salt Lake City: Bookcraft, 1965.

———. *Doctrines of the Restoration: Sermons and Writings of Bruce R. McConkie*. Mark L. McConkie, ed. Salt Lake City: Bookcraft, 1989.

———. *New Witness for the Articles of Faith*. Salt Lake City: Deseret Book, 1985.

McCullough, David. *John Adams*. New York: Simon and Schuster, 2002.

McDonald, David Herbert. *Lincoln*. New York: Simon and Schuster, 1995.

McLaughlin, Andrew Cunningham. *The Foundations of American Constitutionalism*. New York: NYU Press, 1932.

"The Message of the First Presidency to the Church." *Improvement Era*, November 1942, 761.

National Longitudinal Survey of Youth. The Heritage Foundation, 1996.

Nibley, Hugh. *Approaching Zion*. Salt Lake City: Deseret Book, 1989.

Notes of the Debates in the Federal Convention of 1787 Reported by James Madison. Athens, Ohio: Ohio University Press, 1966.

Oaks, Dallin H. "The Great Plan of Happiness." *Ensign*, November 1993, 72–75.

Packer, Boyd K. "Little Children." *Ensign*, November 1986, 16–18.

———. "Self-Reliance." *Ensign*, August 1975, 85–89.

———. *The Things of the Soul*. Salt Lake City: Bookcraft, 1996.

Panati, Charles. *Words to Live By: The Origins of Conventional Wisdom and Commonsense Advice*. New York: Penguin, 1999.

Perry, L. Tom. "Fatherhood, An Eternal Calling." *Ensign*, May 2004, 69–72.

Pratt, Parley P. *Autobiography of Parley P. Pratt*. Revised and enhanced edition. Scot Facer Proctor and Maurine Jensen Proctor, eds. Salt Lake City: Deseret Book, 2000.

———. *Key to the Science of Theology*. Salt Lake City: Deseret Book, 1965.

Sandburg, Carl. *Abraham Lincoln: The Prairie Years and the War Years*. New York: Harcourt Brace, 1954.

Smith, Joseph, Jr. *History of the Church of Jesus Christ of Latter-day Saints*. 7 vols. Salt Lake City: The Church of Jesus Christ of Latter-day Saints, 1932–1951.

———. *Teachings of the Prophet Joseph Smith*. Joseph Fielding Smith, ed. Salt Lake City: Deseret Book, 1976.

Smith, Joseph F. *Gospel Doctrine*. Salt Lake City: Deseret Book, 1939.

Smith, Joseph Fielding. *Doctrines of Salvation*. 3 vols. Bruce R. McConkie, comp. Salt Lake City: Bookcraft, 1954.

———. "Magnifying Our Callings in the Priesthood." *Improvement Era*, June 1970, 65–66.

Smith, Lucy Mack. *The History of Joseph Smith by His Mother*. Revised and enhanced edition. Scot Facer Proctor and Maurine Jensen Proctor, eds. Salt Lake City: Bookcraft, 1996.

Stanley, Thomas J. *The Millionaire Mind*. Kansas City: Andrews McNeel Publishing, 2000.

Talmage, James E. "The Eternity of Sex." *Young Woman's Journal*, October 1914, 602–3.

Taylor, John. *The Gospel Kingdom: Selections from the Writings and Discourses of John Taylor*. G. Homer Durham, ed. Salt Lake City: Deseret Book, 1943.

Teachings of the Presidents of the Church: Heber J. Grant. Salt Lake City: The Church of Jesus Christ of Latter-day Saints, 2003.

Torricelli, Robert, and Andrew Carroll, eds. *In Our Own Words*. New York: Kodansha International, 1999.

Walton, Russ. *Biblical Principles of Importance to Godly Christians*. New Hampshire: Plymouth Foundation, 1984.

Wasserman, Jacob. *Columbus: Don Quixote of the Seas*. Eric Sutton, trans. Boston: Little, Brown, 1930.

Widtsoe, John A. *Evidences and Reconciliations*. Salt Lake City: Bookcraft, 1987.

———. *Priesthood and Church Government*. Salt Lake City: Deseret Book, 1939.

Wilkins, Richard G. "The Social Role of the Family." World Family Policy Center.

Woodruff, Wilford. *Our Lineage: Lessons 1 to 10 of the Course for First Year Senior Genealogical Classes*. Salt Lake City: Genealogical Society of Utah, 1933.

Index

✤